DEAD RECKONINGS

A Review of Horror and the Weird in the Arts
Edited by Alex Houstoun and Michael J. Abolafia

No. 31 (Spring 2022)

DEAD RECKONINGS is published by Hippocampus Press, P.O. Box
641, New York, NY 10156 (www.hippocampuspress. com). Copyright
© 2022 by Hippocampus Press. Cover art by Jason C. Eckhardt. Cover
design by Barbara Briggs Silbert. Hippocampus Press logo by Anastasia
Damianakos. Orders and subscriptions should be sent to Hippocampus
Press. Contact Alex Houstoun at deadreckoningsjournal@gmail.com
for assignments or before submitting a publication for review.

ISSN 1935-6110   ISBN 978-1-61498-375-0

A Swordly and Sorcerous Chronicle

Darrell Schweitzer

BRIAN MURPHY. *Flame and Crimson: A History of Sword-and-Sorcery*. n.p.: Pulp Hero Pres, 2019. 282 pp. $19.95 tpb. ISBN 9781683902447.

Another souvenir from Pulpfest (see *Dead Reckonings* 30). The first thing I will say is that this book needs an index. Like any author, the first thing I did was egoscan this book, i.e. look up what he said about me, since I am, in a very small way, a part of the history being related here. Yes, I am mentioned a couple times. One article by me is cited. My novel *The White Isle* is mentioned on page 210 with my name misspelled. *We Are All Legends* is not mentioned, either because Brian Murphy doesn't know it or because he doesn't think it relevant. (That's his choice.) My *Conan's World and Robert E. Howard* is passed over with merciful silence. . . . But, vanity aside, this book needs an index because it is a serious and substantial work of scholarship, covering an area of literary history largely ignored by academics or critics generally. I will admit that one of its points of interest for me, and the reason I bought the book at Pulpfest is that I myself have struggled for years over some of the same issues addressed here. Such as: What do we mean by sword-and-sorcery anyhow? Is it a valid literary form or merely what Alexei Panshin once called a "literary fossil"? Is it defined by its clichés? I confess that one of the essays of my youth, which I do not intend to reprint, was a piece for the Fantasy Association's journal *Fantasiae* circa 1974 called "Sword and Sorcery: A Wart on the Face of Fair Fantasy?" At the time I was exhibiting the kind of high-falutin' snobbery Murphy so rightly decries; doubly ironic for someone himself guilty of writing what is pretty likely to be considered sword-and-sorcery by any definition.

Definitions are the crux of the matter, for Murphy and for me. The issue is simply this: Is sword-and-sorcery defined by a narrow set of elements, including the muscular barbarian hero, the hero's low or selfish motivations, swordplay, magic, wizards, a scantily clad lady to be rescued, etc.? Is sword-and-sorcery then a subset of epic or heroic fantasy the way the hardboiled detective story is a subset of the mystery story? Both forms are readily defined by a specific paperback cover image, sword-swinging, the fur-loincloth-clad barbarian (usually with ridiculous fur boots) or the detective in the trenchcoat, usually lighting a cigarette, with the brim of his hat turned down. So what if the detective is upper-class and doesn't wear a trenchcoat? What if the barbarian dresses more sensibly, and perhaps isn't quite a barbarian, or uses a crossbow rather than a sword? What if the hero is a skinny adolescent who left his father's magic sword in the attic, never uses anything larger than a small knife, and is himself the sorcerer? (Yes, I wrote that one.) Is sword-and-sorcery then like a hologram that fades away as you remove one element after another?

You could argue that, like any other specialized genre, sword-and-sorcery is what is published under the label. But the label (and what we used to jokingly call "fur jockstrap books") has disappeared, at least from the mass market, so was that the end of it? Brian Murphy comes close to agreeing. He admits sword-and-sorcery has disappeared from the output of major publishers, and today is to be found mostly in the fringes of the small press, in webzines such as *Heroic Fantasy Quarterly* and anthologies such as *Tales from the Magician's Skull*. My own conclusion, to which he more or less concurs, is that it disappeared from the commercial marketplace because, as the various elements were taken away, the form was replaced by multi-volume sagas like those of George R. R. Martin or Robert Jordan. In other words, Panshin was wrong. Sword-and-sorcery did evolve, but into something else.

Murphy's definition is more a matter of "low" vs. "high" fantasy. In a sword-and-sorcery story the hero (a barbarian or outsider of some sort) has no lofty or noble purpose. He is not out to save the world. He is not a hidden king-in-waiting like Tolkien's Aragorn. His motivations are smaller, usually selfish, and often morally ambivalent, like those of the characters in Glen Cook's Dark Company series, who may be on the "wrong" side, but that's where the money is, and historians can sort out the right and wrong of it later. The hero is physically strong, but his triumph, insofar as there is one, is a matter of the strength of his will. The operative models for this sort of thing are the Conan series by Robert E. Howard and the Fafhrd and Gray Mouser series by Fritz Leiber. Murphy also notes that sword-and-sorcery adventures also tend to be short, either novelettes, like the Conan series, or single-volume novels. While Michael Moorcock's Elric saga may seem to violate this, each Elric book is self-standing, rather than part of a single, sprawling story that goes on for volume after volume as is the case with George R. R. Martin or Robert Jordan.

Given this premise, Murphy quite competently follows the development of sword-and-sorcery from its antecedents and root-texts (arguing that Robert E. Howard was far more influenced by swashbuckling historical novels than by the fantasies of Lord Dunsany or William Morris) and finding the true point of origin (as many of us have) in Howard's "The Shadow Kingdom" (1926), in which all the elements were assembled for the first time. Conan of course follows. Then comes a generation after Howard, with Henry Kuttner's Elak of Atlantis, Leiber's Fafhrd and Mouser, etc. C. L. Moore is acknowledged as an important contemporary of Howard; her influence, great as it is, would have been even greater if she had written more than five Jirel of Joiry stories. This history takes us through the 1950s (where the highlight is Poul Anderson's *The Broken Sword*) and into the "boom" period of the 1960s and '70s following the publication of the Lancer Conan books (and the controversies surrounding them), and ultimately on to a flood-of-crud and the collapse of the field, as it was replaced commercially by the Martin/Jordan/Terry Brooks sort of fantasy series. There are good chapters on the influence of sword-and-sorcery in other media, such as film, heavy metal music, and gaming. He seems to take the original *Conan the Barbarian* movie (1982) a lot more seriously than I do, I will admit, and if that is the high standard to which nothing else measures up (indeed, the later films sound mostly awful; based on those I have seen, I can confirm that they are), then I think I will just watch *Jason and the Argonauts* again, thank you.

This is the kind of book you can have a friendly argument with. I've never met Brian Murphy, but I am sure we'd have a lot to talk about if I ever did. In that light, I have my "nitpicking" list, which I compiled as I read *Flame and Crimson*. This is small stuff, which does not invalidate the book in any way. Some of it is just proofreading, such as that Ursula Le Guin's name is consistently misspelled throughout. (Not "LeGuin." Space after the "Le.") It is mildly irritating that one-author collections are frequently described as "anthologies." It is also trivial to note that Queen Victoria died in 1901, which means that Lord Dunsany published no fiction, only one poem, in the Victorian Age. A bit more substantially, while the discussion of the Howard/Lovecraft "civilization vs. barbarism" debate provides much insight into Robert E. Howard's thinking, it fails to note that Lovecraft's "fascism" had morphed into an odd form of "socialism" by the mid-1930s. (Around 1936 you can find HPL the Red discussing with Kenneth Sterling whether the Russian Revolution was a good idea, and how necessary socialism may be achieved in the United States.) On page 95, Murphy repeats the old saw that C. L. Moore used initials to hide her gender and only mentions in a footnote that others "theorize" that this had something to do with her hiding her writing income from her boss at the bank. No, this is not a theory. It was what Moore herself said over and over again for the rest of her life. Page 103: By the time Fritz Leiber was publishing in *Astounding* the title had been changed from *Astounding Stories* to the somewhat more dignified *Astounding Science Fiction*. Page 136: Among "mimeographed fanzines" are listed *Witchcraft and Sorcery, Chacal, Escape,* and even *Amra*. While *Amra* fit anyone's definition of a fanzine, it was outstanding for its (never mimeographed) printing and graphics. *Witchcraft and Sorcery* was (for at least two issues anyway) a full-blown (if underfinanced) prozine, distributed on newsstands and an obvious attempt to replace *Weird Tales. Chacal* was a very professional-looking magazine with color covers and high-quality printing and design, and distributed in bookstores. *Escape,* I can tell you as a contributor (I had two stories in the one and only issue), was typeset and glossy. It and *Chacal* both published original Karl Edward Wagner stories. Both were high-end small-press magazines, certainly as "professional" as any we have today.

Page 145: Poul Anderson's celebrated "The Barbarian" is not an "essay" but a short story, one of the first professional Conan parodies. Has Murphy actually read this? Much more importantly, he seems to think that the Karl Edward Wagner edited "pure text" Conan volumes published by Berkley were wickedly suppressed by L. Sprague de Camp. Like many Howard fans, he has issues with de Camp. How flawed is *Dark Valley Destiny*? Were the editorial changes de Camp made to Howard's texts in the Lancer Conans worth doing? Did de Camp for many years perpetuate a false image of Robert E. Howard himself and his work? Fans will argue all that for years to come. But as far as I can tell, what actually happened to the Wagner-edited Conans was a bit more complex. There was a lot of money at stake. The movie people wanted to get going with *Conan the Barbarian* and they needed to clear the rights immediately. This was no time for squabbles, in or out of a courtroom. So the interested parties got together, formed Conan Properties Inc., and divided up the rights to the satisfaction of all, which meant that the Lancer/Ace de Camp–edited Conan series would continue and the Berkley series would not. Glenn Lord was left in charge of all other Howard material, but CPI henceforth controlled the Conan franchise. Wagner was left to write Conan pastiche novels, which he did. The movie could proceed.

This is indeed the kind of stuff we could talk about at conventions endlessly. But no such quibbles seriously detract from the overall excellence of *Flame and Crimson,* which very capably maps out the territory, and provides the basis for all such future discussions. It is highly recommended.

One Pure Writer's Will

Michael D. Miller

FARAH ROSE SMITH. *Of One Pure Will*. Carbondale, IL: Trepidatio Publishing, 2021. 177 pp. $14.00 tpb. ISBN: 978-1685100018.

> "Survivors of great horror often speak of the angst, the apprehension, the instinct within that warned them of their impending experience. They wade into the story with descriptions about the sights and sounds, and with maddening optimism spin it in some way so maybe even they can handle reliving it all. Am I guilty of this? Without question."
> —Farah Rose Smith, "The Land of Other"

Farah Rose Smith is no stranger to this journal, having her own work reviewed here while also writing reviews of other writers and interviewed at length for the now-defunct *Mantid* project for women writers of horror. She has three novellas to her credit: *ANONYMA, The Almanac of Dust,* and *Eviscerator*. Her scholarly work has appeared in a variety of literary journals and conferences, and she also serves as a part-time literary agent. She has won multiple festival awards for screenwriting. In addition to these credentials, Farah Rose Smith is an active presence on social media, creating a doorway into her personal outlook, opinions, and tragedies, all bearing an impact that is hard to separate.

On this idea of an author's personality and worldview obviously apparent in the work, one is reminded of Harlan Ellison, whose hallmark was to distill his personality into the fiction to the point where the writing was him just as much as the story. If you follow Farah Rose Smith on Twitter long enough to get a sense of her aesthetic, you will see that the work is such a product of the writer's personality that you know no one else could have produced it. While many readers do not respond to this, those who do (including me) find that it empowers authors' work with a unique stamp of their own voice. In the introduction to this collection Jeffrey Thomas notices as much, stating: "Separating voice from writing is like separating voice from song, and many singers have unique voices indeed, to be savored. [Farah Rose Smith] sings from a shared unconsciousness that we all recognize by its unknowable vastness." I would agree to a point, the voice of this work is not separated from the writer by any means, and it is different, decadent, and "trapped in a dream-disease."

Reviewing *Of One Pure Will,* labeled "a collection," we might ask, "A collection of what?" Perhaps a quest for the truly weird. The contents contain forays into many subgenres: body horror, psychological horror, and even dream horror. In practice almost all the stories are evocative of dream-logic. You don't know what to expect. No promises. A trip through the middle, non-traditional, non-linear, and with few exceptions, no "beginning" and no "end." I therefore utilized a new technique with this collection, reviewing as I read through it, rather than unpacking the whole. In that way it is impossible to mention or do justice (not to mention overwhelming on all fronts for the reader) to cite every work in *Of One Pure Will,* so I will be focusing on a few standout tales below.

One essential element permeating all the stories of worth is prose style and story titles. Smith's prose recalls classic and new Gothic stylists such as M. R. James, Walter de la Mare, Lewis Carroll, William Hope Hodgson, Edgar Allan Poe, and even W. H. Pugmire, yet remains an acquired taste all its own. Titles such as "The Wytch-Byrd of the Nabyrd-Keind," "In the Way of Eslan Mendeghast," and "Time Disease (In the Waking City)" hone that point. Descriptions are rich and fresh. One wonders where did this come from? What time period? "Eight cages have arrived on the doorstep of Emiel Forsa. Eight immaculate, iron-wrought contraptions in wedding-white. The contents are invisible, hidden behind a translucent sheath of fabric woven between the bars, glittering with microscopic breathing holes pierced by sewing needle." Or: "Anguish was her predicament. And now she feasted on a broken treaty of the Afterworld, fluttering and writhing with these visions like the loathsome ghouls found beneath those ancient lands." Characters are given equally stylistic descriptions: "Forsa thinks himself trapped in a dream-disease. The necrotic-REM of self-annihilation . . . an effortless haunt . . . He is painted from within by his torment" and "A frozen form so like Rook in the land of dreams, in the throes of flesh-melt; the highest form of dream transfiguration." Perhaps fitting this style, the narratives are not structured plots but simple moments that fade out between each other like old silent films.

In "In the Way of Eslan Mendeghast" the narrative is second-person poetry, often unintelligible, and most won't get it, but perhaps we don't need to. The overall effect, being more important than story, is accomplished like a stream-of-consciousness rabbit (or worm) hole. The folktale-like nature of "Eslan Mendeghast" is on par with a good run for *Baba Yaga* in one of the characters, Olag Kengkhovra, with an equally compelling atmosphere as if Dunsany were writing *The King of Elfland's Daughter* in second-person. The stories, and this one, are not really *stories* in the true sense but *experiences* and a perhaps better initiation into the world of Farah Rose Smith. They all have attentive mood-setting openings: "This is the fourth time you have chased Eslan Mendeghast out into the Moors, and it will be your last." The "dream-lands" of this and other stories are swamps, woodlands, and mires, all dissolved of the modern world and its bullshit. They make for effective mood and atmosphere yet sometimes fall into opacity, like the "too dark cinematography" trend we've seen in *Game of Thrones,* the *Batman* franchise, and others—we get some of it, but the rest is unclear. I can't recommend much of the collection as good traditional weird fiction, but I can recommend many stories in the collection, such as "Mendeghast," as worthy experiences of what that should or could possibly be. Decadent—too much so to be perfect.

"The Visitor" is an entirely different experience of body horror on par with some of the best Cronenberg films or this year's Palme d'Or winner, *Titane.* There is a veneer of pretentiousness to this story that fits because it's a story of "rock 'n' roll." As a rock-myth type iconography there is a "rebirth" theme to this story. The basic fabric is set up in the opening paragraph:

Aimee loves "Rookie Swallows." The pounding of the opening riff. That melt-your-insides, wet-the-inner-sanctum drive. Every time she hears it, she tilts her head back and takes a swig of the rotting air. Blue veins in her neck pulse to the pounding of the drums *boom boom boom*. Miller watches a drop of sweat roll down her chest through the haze–liquid pink. One more puff, one more go around the turnstile . . .

Rook and Miller are in a band, there are sex and drugs as well, Miller overdosing soon after and being possessed by the beast of "the Visitor," taking over the corpse of Miller, the band, and Rook's soul. The essential weirdness of this tale occurs during the tour: with the beast in charge, he takes Rook's soul and body on a hypnagogic journey of transfiguration to the afterworld. The Visitor describes it as "a man who finds himself a wanderer between doomed worlds. He indulges in one, and saves the other. Temptation leads him to make quite the mess! If that doesn't have the making of a tragic masterpiece, I don't know what does." The tragedy, of course, is all on Rook. Many won't connect with most of what happens here, as the vision is too personal to draw everyone in. That might be okay, but still the question, what is this? remains. Perhaps that is the point of the collection as most of the stories end this way. Yet it does make a reader think about the writing for a time after the last page is turned.

"The Land of Other," which weaves a fine subtle tribute to Emily Dickinson with a window-view of the world, is not a story but a psychological dream state—decadent expressionism about disability stigma. Voice and passion are most clear in this story, a Farah Rose Smith afterworld. But really the denouement structure is more of a reflection once again than a traditional story, but in 2022 so what? As for the Emily Dickinson mood, our narrator's view outside is: "There are no sights free from the garnish of torment. Not anymore. No sweetness free from the grip of the ice, choking me with the burden of these remembrances." It is the story of a recently recovered woman, a survivor, still stricken from an accident and the losses surrounding the event. One of the losses was her cherished horse, shipped off to retirement in her youth, yet haunting her to this moment. The other tragedy involves her son, Oliver, whom she can't remember, and the agony of triumphing over disability. The impact of that to her is a desire for the land of the other. This is one of the most passionate of stories, and the narrator has some perfect revelations of the painful path to recovery. "This is the first step towards the Land of the Other. The gift of the senses to that unknown, endless realm. It watches on, even now." "The greater fear, living outside the shame of this, is the idea I will someday remember." "My brain grips the eons of a strange, infirm ever after. I will not be without it now." These all confront her as a failing mother and the nature of ableism. In the end, her doctor assures her of a full "physical" recovery. The land of other still beckons her as well, forever. Some problems are that the beats are not synched very well, and it would help to rein in the fragmenting episodes to some degree. This narrative (and others) seems to ask, what is the line between prose and poetry?

"A Delirium of Mothers: Based on a True Story" could have been a ballad on Harry Smith's *American Folk Music Anthology* for sheer mood and atmosphere alone. This tale is an effective example of mother horror—the loss of a child with a strong theme of survival running through the plot. While it does mimic certain aspects of Stephen King's *Pet Cemetery,* it holds its own voice. Carter and Riyah Dordevic move into a rural farmhouse built in 1887 after Riyah's undiagnosed miscarriage in September 1994. Carter narrates the tale as they explore the homestead seeking solace. They discover an unmarked grave on the premises, learn from an elderly neighbor, Mitchell Mauvis, that it's the grave of Sarah Hanner, dead a hundred years ago from suicide. Thereafter Riyah begins to relive the trauma of loss, believing she is at fault for Sarah's death, and a haunting presence begins to take its toll on the married couple. As most ghost-folk stories do, it tests the bounds on the family unit. "A Delirium of Mothers" is also one of the few traditional stories where we have a beginning-middle-end of a sort, though it feels open-ended enough to be more of a first chapter of a longer narrative.

The shifting nature of collections—too long, too short, too scattered—is not new but they often contain gems. And so does *Of One Pure Will*. If you need a break from all the monotony . . . if you want to immerse for a time in language . . . if you want the deepest Gothic sickness brought out of your own unconsciousness . . . this is for you. The narratives are maddening and frustrating at times, perhaps too much so. I don't know ultimately what to conclude as a final review of this work other than it is indeed of one pure will!

A Laudable Gem

Géza A. G. Reilly

ALEX HOUSTOUN. *Copyright Questions and the Stories of H. P. Lovecraft*. Self-published, 2021. 75 pp. No ISBN.

One of the joys of participating in a community of fans, scholars, and professionals is having access to texts that might otherwise slip by unnoticed and unlauded. Alex Houstoun's *Copyright Questions and the Stories of H. P. Lovecraft* is one such text: it is a small chapbook, independently prepared and published, that is nonetheless insightful and illuminating of a subject that has been the point of contentious debate among Lovecraft aficionados for years. If Houstoun continues to release his *Copyright Questions* or allows it to be picked up by a publisher proper, which is a route I would heartily endorse, then I would easily recommend that anyone interested in the question of who actually owns the stories of H. P. Lovecraft (specifically the stories he published in *Weird Tales* magazine during his lifetime) buy a copy.

The question of ownership of Lovecraft's published work has been a conundrum for decades. The most common preconception on the matter, which is one that I subscribed to for years, is that after Lovecraft's death the copyright to his works would have been transferred to Annie Gamwell, Lovecraft's surviving aunt and closest relative. August Derleth and Donald Wandrei, however, facetiously claimed copyright ownership of Lovecraft's stories and poetry (and ideas therein) after the establishment of Arkham House, their publishing firm. They then defended these erroneous copyright claims with threats of court action on several occasions, which led to situations like the infamous 1980 case of role-playing game company Chaosium, to whom Arkham House had licensed Lovecraft's creations, legally threatening competitor TSR for including those creations in their (also Arkham House–licensed) sourcebook *Deities and Demigods*. After the death of

August Derleth and the revelations of Lovecraft criticism in the mid-to-late 1970s, however, the truth came out and Lovecraft's work was inching toward being public domain—which occurred, depending on who you asked at the time, anywhere between the 1990s and the 2010s.

Houstoun brilliantly works through how right and wrong these preconceptions are in his slim 75-page chapbook. Everything he lays out, from human concerns, to noted characters, to bad decisions, to legal precedents, builds upon one another to explode commonly held positions within and without fandom. I will not reveal his conclusions here, since there are as many twists and turns in his essay as there are in a good courtroom drama (including one absolutely mind-blowing connection to a twenty-first century television sitcom), but suffice it to say that I had no earthly way to answer the Lovecraft copyright question in the manner that Houstoun has. Admittedly, I am not a lawyer, but Houstoun is, and he has made a case in such a way that I cannot imagine either professionals or laymen finding his work unpersuasive. Indeed, I would say that Houstoun's investigation of the ownership of Lovecraft's stories sheds a whole new light on copyright in general for laymen and how such a conception has operated within the American system over the past hundred-odd years.

When I referred to Houstoun's chapbook as an "essay," I was being quite literal. The text began its life as an independent study in law school and was written in the manner of a law journal article. While this did not stick out to me in any way (despite having next to no experience of law journals in general), it must be said that some readers may find the text a bit dry at times, somewhat internally self-referential, and generally unemotional in the writing itself. This is by design, however; after all, *Copyright Questions* is not a bombastic editorial nor a simple opinion piece. It is, in the manner of the best of academic texts, an earnest attempt at determining the facts of the matter and nothing more. To that end, it might not be a gripping page-turner for some, but for those who are curious about discovering the intricacies of the situation, no other format would have been quite so satisfying.

To be sure, Houstoun is not the first to investigate the

matter of Lovecraft's copyrights, and he does make space for noting where he is building off the work of others (most notably, George Wetzel, Chris J. Karr, and, to some extent, S. T. Joshi). He is, however, the only one to come up with what seems to be (and I only include that "seems" because I am, again, no lawyer myself) a definitive answer to the question once and for all. Indeed, after much rumination, I could not find a single reason to doubt Houstoun's conclusions despite my own preferences for the state of Lovecraft publishing. *Copyright Questions* is, then, a satisfying end point for the question that has puzzled Lovecraft fans and scholars for years, and it is an example of the best kind of investigative academic writing: It states its case, provides its evidence, presents its findings, and parachutes out before things become overwrought.

It would be a crying shame if more members of the Lovecraft/horror community at large went unaware of Houstoun's laudable work. Indeed, as I said at the outset, one of the joys of being a member of these communities is the opportunity to experience and appreciate the independent work of others who followed their passions for no reason other than that they could. *Copyright Questions and the Stories of H. P. Lovecraft* is one such passion project, and it is a gem of its kind. I wholeheartedly recommend it to any fan of Lovecraft, or even anyone who wants a short crash course on the operations of sometimes arcane American copyright law. This is not a work that should slip easily into the darkness of obscurity; it should be on all our shelves. And if any publishers happen to be reading this review, well, you could do worse than to send Alex Houstoun a quick email to ensure that it could be.

Men in Pain

Javier Martinez

JEFFREY THOMAS. *Carrion Men*. Edited by Scott Dwyer. n.p.: Plutonian Press, 2020. 212 pp. $11.50 tpb. ISBN: 979-8580702452.

Carrion Men brings together six stories and a novella by Jeffrey Thomas. In his editor's introduction Scott Dwyer refers to these stories as some his personal favorites, making this collection not so much a new addition to Thomas's overall body of work as a curated product that showcases tales that speak to Dwyer, in part because of their "focus on broken and beaten up men, men corrupted and diseased . . . men being devoured from within, eaten alive by this strange existence and the even stranger bodies we find ourselves inhibiting [*sic*]." (Dwyer obviously means "inhabiting," but the use of "inhibiting" is an intuitive slip.) The collection closes with an essay by Joshua Dinges, a somewhat autobiographical reflection piece that nevertheless provides some real insight into Thomas's recurring themes. Like Dwyer, Dinges notes how these stories focus on men, specifically men who are "beset on all sides by feelings of loneliness and alienation. They are plagued by a sense of familial loss. They are middle-aged men with widening middles, working or laid off from middling jobs." With the focus of this collection on the male experience, specifically the white male experience, as is clearly stated in the critical pieces that bookend the stories, the overall sense that I take away from *Carrion Men* is that it is positioned naggingly out of the context of the current literary moment. At a time when genre fiction is expanding to include the experiences of a wide spectrum of non-traditional bodies and agencies, why do we need this collection that is so specifically focused on male characters?

I want to be clear that I am not disqualifying the need or importance of this collection. Rather, what I am looking for and not finding is a contextualization of the work. Where does the editor see Thomas's work in relation to the work of other authors of a different gender working in the same field? I think this is a fair question to ask. After all, it is the editor who has chosen consciously and systematically these male-centric stories. And just to restate my prior assertion, I am fine with a gender-centric approach, but such an approach needs to take place with an understanding, or at least an acknowledgment, that such a focused endeavor necessarily occurs within a larger plurality that it cannot be excised from. The dis-ease I felt reading this collection was created not only by Thomas's stories (and I mean this as a compliment to Thomas), but by the lack of reflexivity that such a curated volume needs to be a truly robust contribution to the field.

I share Dwyer's enthusiasm and admiration for Jeffrey Thomas. I do not wish to be too harsh on Dwyer. If he wants to put together a personal greatest hits of one of his favorite authors, and if he has the resources to do it, then by all means proceed. But this collection could have, and should have, been stronger. As such, it is something of a missed opportunity.

But I have spent too much time railing against an editor whose intentions are obviously good, and who has put together a decent if limited sampling of Thomas's unique work. We have Dwyer to thank, after all, for bringing into print for the first time two stories never before published. "The Crying Boy" and "Last Cup of Sorrow" are original to this collection, and the latter may be, along with "Scorpion Face," the strongest of the bunch.

"Last Cup of Sorrow" and "Scorpion Face" are the highlights of the collection. "Last Cup of Sorrow" places the reader in a near-future world that has been colonized by translucent quasi-organic dog-like creatures that consume the life essence of people. Those hunted down by the dogs awaken hours later to find themselves aged by decades. The protagonist, impersonally named Suit, a generic everyman character, has an intuitive but unclear understanding that the dogs are not native to the world, evoking some dimly understood moment of colonization that fundamentally altered human life. But just what happened and why are questions left tantalizingly unanswered.

"Scorpion Face" is an experimental story of sorts that

chronicles the banal existence of two characters, John and the titular Scorpion Face. John works as a low-level employee tasked with fielding customer complaints. He spends his days tracking down lost packages and his evenings masturbating on online forums. Scorpion Face, John's counterpart in an alternate dimension, is a scorpion-like creature that spends his days in similar banal tasks, rerouting creatures that resemble working ants through a series of tunnels. In the evenings Scorpion Face indulges in frantic and unfulfilling sexual congress with its neighbor via marionettes. John holds a pistol to his head every evening but is unable to pull the trigger. Scorpion Face, on the other hand, can follow through with its attempts at suicide but finds itself coming back to life at the start of every workday. Both protagonists are doomed to live out the same pattern for the rest of their lives. "Scorpion Face" is a remarkably efficient and focused story that successfully distills the very best qualities of Thomas's weirdness into a powerful draught of despair and isolation. "Last Cup of Sorrow" is a welcome return to the horror-tinged science fiction that long-time Thomas readers have seen in his Punktown series.

"The Crying Boy" is the other story original to this collection, but it lacks the power of "Last Cup of Sorrow." It is not a bad story; indeed, it has one of the best conceits of any Thomas story to date: the reflection cast by the protagonist, named Manning, is always that of himself as a six-year-old, crying. The story highlights the sexual tension between him and his cousin Dawn, six years his junior. Disturbingly, there is an implication that something occurred between them when Manning was six and Dawn an infant. Manning has psychologically never moved past that moment, even now as a man more than twenty years later. The story shifts in another direction, however, painting Manning as an insane artist more concerned with his art than with human life. The result is that "The Crying Boy" feels more like an idea that Thomas decided not to follow up on, consciously or not; and given the subject matter, this might be for the best. Still, from a purely aesthetic perspective the story fails to gel.

"Carrion" finds the protagonist Lambert obsessing over both a female co-worker and the rotting roadkill he passes on the way to work every morning. When his colleague's pregnancy begins to show, Lambert notices something moving inside the carcass. In time, the unborn child and the oversize beetle-like thing gnawing its way through the dead animal on the road merge in Lambert's mind as a singular entity, probably non-corporeal but possibly not, that lives within us all, eating away at us in a psychic if not physical sense. This type of story, where there is a thing in question that may or may not be real and that may or may not materialize and which may or may not have real effects, can be difficult to pull off, and "Carrion" does not find its mark.

Neither does "The Prosthesis." Originally published in *The Grimscribe's Puppets,* a tribute anthology to Thomas Ligotti, the story follows a character named Thomas, who works in a factory that manufactures prosthesis and replacement limbs. Thomas is haunted by a memory of once having been chased down a tunnel by a lumbering, hunched figure always obscured by darkness. Early in the story it is revealed that Thomas had a twin brother, Mason, who died at birth, prompting one of the best lines in the collection: "I've always mourned somebody I never knew." The inconsolable sadness of that line is intense and powerful. The story, however, does not satisfactorily bring its various threads together. Readers of the weird will recognize this story's qualities as Ligotti-ish, as befitting the purpose of its original publication venue, but Ligotti and Jeffrey Thomas are at heart very different writers, even if they share an affinity for the grotesque. In that sense, the imagery in "The Prosthesis" is effective and memorable, but the story reads as if the author is writing in such a way that he is chaffing against his own natural inclinations.

"The Tangible Universe," however, is much more successful. The tangible universe of the title is a museum of human oddities, with each oddity displaying only his or her affliction, disfigurement, or deformity, which the protagonist sees as individual worlds in a universe of physical deviance, all the while remaining behind a partition that hides the rest of their unblemished bodies. What makes this story so effective is that it displays Thomas's strengths as a writer—his ability to materialize the grotesque in ways that begin as abstractions but move inexorably toward realization and communion. Put another way, Thomas's horror is created by a process that is the exact opposite of that employed by Ligotti, whose horrors become increasingly abstract and psychical as the story progresses. Thomas's signature focus on deviant desire and sexual grotesquerie is on full display here, but as in his best work it is never used for merely prurient purposes, rather as a natural culmination of the character arc that he has crafted for us.

"Door 7" is the longest piece in the collection and the only one told in first person. An unnamed narrator tours an abandoned factory, all the while musing philosophically and pushing a stroller that holds his deceased son's favorite doll, Grover from *Sesame Street*. As he moves deeper into the factory, each subsequent door presents a new grotesque revelation that builds on the one before. The story culminates in the narrator giving birth to his dead son, who hatches from a tumor that has grown on the left side of his head. I had previously commented on "Door 7" in my review of Thomas's *Thirteen Specimens* for this journal (No. 7, Spring 2010). After re-reading the novella, I find that my original reaction to the story has not changed:

> Thomas seems to revel in his gruesome imagery. Thomas very effectively crafts some disturbing scenes, but their impact is not enough to sustain a story that is mired in the same kind of narrative confusion that spoils the experience the author does such a fine job of cultivating [in other stories]. "Mask Play" and "Door 7" are not bad stories. They might even be taken as competent examples of the art if they had been written by anyone else. The stories simply cannot stand with some of the stronger pieces in the collection, and when placed beside them they come across as lacking.

And there I think is the culminating statement on this collection. Except for "Last Cup of Sorrow," "Scorpion Face," and "The Tangible Universe," *Carrion Men* does not represent the best that Thomas has to offer. Granted, no collection is without its lesser stories, but in the case of a curated collection the purpose of *Carrion Men* seems lost to me. Who exactly is this meant for? Those new to Thomas's work will not find a good entry to it here, and those familiar with his work will not find his best here. Perhaps what this collection accomplishes best is that it raises the issue that perhaps it is time for someone to put together a true "Best of" collection of Thomas's stories, something that will serve as a gateway for newcomers and something that will give longtime readers a critical and historical overview of Thomas's strongest and most distinctive work.

The "Weird" in Isolation: An Interview with Gordon B. White

David Peak

Many of the creative people I know have struggled during the COVID-19 pandemic. Some have lost motivation in the face of wave after wave of nightmarish news stories and shocking statistics; others have turned to distractions for comfort. Still others—perhaps the lucky few—have interrogated the anxieties of recent months and created stories and art that reflect a world forever changed.

Gordon B. White, who wrote and released his first book-length work of fiction, *Rookfield* (Trepidatio Publishing), during the pandemic, is one of these lucky few. The story centers on Cabot Howard, whose ex-wife has taken his young son and fled to the titular town. There, the townspeople are strangely insistent on mask protocol, no one seems to know anything, and there are whisperings of strange rituals. To White's credit, the folk-tinged, stranger-comes-to-town narrative is always compelling, recalling the best elements of *Silent Hill* and *The Wicker Man*.

What makes *Rookfield* particularly special, however, is how its story tackles the complications of COVID-19. Plague-doctor masks figure heavily into the story and have thematic resonance. Townspeople are distrustful of outsiders in a way that feels informed by recent events. And human weakness, selfishness, and short-sightedness not only help set the story in motion but also lead to a memorable and ultimately disturbing take on the weird in an increasingly isolated world.

The following interview was conducted by email from October to December 2021.

David Peak: Recently I've seen a few comments about how writers are seemingly ignoring the pandemic in their fiction. That's obviously not the case with *Rookfield*. Did you set out to write a story in response to the pandemic? Or did the pandemic find its way into your story?

Gordon White: While I didn't make an initial decision to write about the pandemic and then set off in search of an idea, *Rookfield*'s central premise emerged from everything that was going on in the spring and early summer of 2020. Sometime during the first lockdown, my good friend Rebecca J. Allred and I were tossing around possible story ideas for some call for submissions I've now forgotten. The pandemic was still new and scary (as opposed to being old and scary), and so it gradually seeped into our pitches. Rebecca has also been making visual art using plague-doctor-esque "Plagues" for years, and so that aesthetic was also swirling around. At some point, these influences got so thoroughly mixed together that an early version of the unique way a town like Rookfield might handle COVID-19 emerged. Without spoiling anything, the central weirdness of *Rookfield* came first, but once it did, I knew I had to write a story to fit it.

While that central strangeness itself is not specific to COVID-19, the rest of the story came together based on what was going on in the world. I've always liked stories that have characters who are isolated or under siege, especially when that isolation isn't just the product of locked doors or high walls, so it seemed fitting to start with a man on an empty highway, driving toward a town that didn't want him there, alone and set apart because of the virus. As I followed him, however, and put him up into conflict with other people, I began to see that the real cause of his isolation wasn't the externalities of the pandemic, but something deeper, something ugly that I saw coming out more and more in people as the restrictions continued.

David: On that point, there aren't a lot of likable people in *Rookfield*—including the main character, Cabot Howard. Were you concerned at all about how readers might react?

Gordon: My concern was to make Cabot a believable and compelling character—and purposefully not a likable one.

However, in the back of my mind I thought about how that unlikability was going to be a barrier to entry for some readers. I've seen that come to pass in some of the reviews and comments since the book's release, although thankfully not as many as I'd feared.

Cabot was intended to be a man of constant action, but one who exists in a world where his every action is wrong. His resilience and resourcefulness might almost be admirable, if he wasn't constantly making everything worse for himself, his loved ones, and anyone who runs into him. He comes from a long line of male protagonists who have a goal and are endlessly creative in their attempts to achieve it, but where Cabot finds himself—in a pandemic, in a family dispute, in a town whose people and practices he won't even try to understand—these are not even remotely the right circumstances for his outmoded, masculine-coded concept of heroism to work.

That said, I did try to give Cabot some nuance so that he wasn't merely a dickhead or a buffoon. He thinks what he's doing is right—even noble—although it should be clear to the reader that this isn't objectively true. Cabot isn't necessarily cruel, but he is self-centered. There's a very purposeful gulf between his perception of himself as almost an action hero under increasingly difficult odds versus the reader's view of him as increasingly bedraggled and unhinged.

David: *Rookfield* is very much centered on the horror of human behavior but gradually builds up to something much larger and more disturbing. Are your stories typically inspired by what you see happening in the world?

Gordon: I think that my stories are inspired by what I see happening in the world, as I don't usually have a fantastical imagination, so the seeds of even the weirdest things are actually pretty mundane. There are a few outliers, but I think a lot of my stories start off as "say what you see but add a scare," and then get run through the telephone game of artistic inspiration and aesthetic refinement for enough circuits to distort them in a—hopefully—fresh way.

Which is to say that my stories very much grow from what

I see (or read or dream), but I don't think there's an explicitly conscious drive to do that. I'm not purposefully rejecting the more fantastical approach or setting out to talk about the world as I see it; it's just that I don't usually have as much interest in the work of *world building* as I do in *world shifting*. I find the real world and the people in it to be endlessly fascinating, and so the characters that walk across my mental stage and the circumstances they find themselves in are usually recognizable, but they just get their dramatic potential cranked up to eleven by a weird or horrific element.

David: I was really impressed by your recent piece "Gordon B. White is creating Haunting Weird Horror" (tinyurl.com/2p8n5xcn), in which a nameless person receives monthly postcards from the author Gordon B. White. Each postcard contains a description of "lesser-known haunted houses," and the overall effect is essentially an overflow of those weird and horrific elements. What inspired you to write this particular story?

Gordon: I'm a big fan of unique structures and formalistic constraints as a method to inspire creativity. The genesis of that one was a desire to write a second-person story, since the (incorrect) common wisdom that gets thrown around is that second-person stories don't sell. Also, I knew I was aiming for flash fiction, and while most stories of that length rely on twists at the end, I wanted to—as you say—get an "overflow" of elements. From there, a couple of random influences swimming around in my subconscious found their way into this structural bottle—namely, Nicole Cushing's Patreon perks, which involve monthly odd doodles, Jeffrey Ford's use of a fictional "Jeff Ford" as a character, and my attempt to get some of the surreal grotesqueness of Matthew M. Bartlett. Then lightning struck. There's a bit (bite?) of humor to this one, too, and I did think as I wrote it, "This might be a good one to add to the live reading repertoire." To that end, I tried really hard to get the voice and flow just right.

David: Let's talk a bit more about your writing process. You're a careful writer and rewriter and you freely share details and advice on your craft online. What was it like working on a longer work with *Rookfield,* and how has that been different from writing short fiction?

Gordon: Over my writing life, I have tried to internalize the idea that each story demands its own process and what works for one story won't necessarily work for another. For a good stretch during the sophomore phase of my writing career, I got very bogged down by writing methods and tools, to the point where any imbalance could mean the creative juices wouldn't flow. I realize now that rituals can be a form of procrastination, certainly for me, but it took a lot of work toward intentionally de-fetishizing the writing process before I could once again do it consistently.

With the pandemic and lockdown—not to mention my burgeoning lack of faith in humanity that had been bubbling over since 2016—I was in a rough place in the early summer of 2020. In an attempt to find some measure of peace and control in an uncontrollable world, I decided to write a short story about a jerk in a plague who gets his comeuppance. However, I decided to try doing it in the lowest-pressure way possible: I committed to writing every day, but the only requirement was that it be in longhand and at least one sentence. That's it. The first day of drafting *Rookfield* became what's now the opening paragraph, and I remember it was just a few sentences, no more than 75 words total. And I could maintain that no-pressure pace, although some days I would literally write a single sentence before bed. Still, I had set the bar low, and so it was a victory.

Building on this streak day by day, and keeping the story moving forward, built up an unexpected momentum. By the time I hit the climax, I wrote it all by hand in one afternoon on my porch, getting sunburned in the process. When I finished, though, I realized I could never amputate enough to fit it into the 5,000-word box of a short story. The only way forward was to build it up and out. I had never done that before and the idea of writing something that long had scared me into immobility in the past, but by that point I'd been working on *Rookfield* consistently for weeks and had come to know the place and characters well enough that I actually wouldn't mind spending another month or more with them. With that realization, those past fears evaporated.

David: How are your views of the pandemic and your faith in humanity holding up as we enter into 2022? What's next on the horizon for you?

Gordon: I'm not sure how things are holding up, to be honest. We have a new variant spreading. Isolation and fatigue seem to have worn down most of us. It seems like this might not ever end, but instead become just a regular tragedy that people—particularly in the United States—just accept as the cost for having this childish infatuation with not being told what to do. See also gun violence, climate change, and a lack of basic housing or medical needs. I don't know if I think the issue is with "humanity," as I still believe that people are capable of great kindness, compassion, and resilience. However, I think the current systems we have in place have failed miserably.

As for what's next, this year sees the release of a new novella I co-wrote with my good friend Rebecca J. Allred, called *And in Her Smile, the World* (JournalStone Publishing). I also have a few short fiction projects lined up for the coming year. Having now successfully tackled two book-length works of fiction, I'm also broadening my horizons. I have an old draft of a novel that I've strapped to the operating table and am now poking about, trying to decide if it's worth fixing up or just breaking down for parts. And I'm also looking forward to beginning a new novel project this year. But I don't want to say too much, for fear of jinxing it.

Ramsey's Rant: From Life

Ramsey Campbell

Some reviews of *The Searching Dead,* the first volume of my Brichester Mythos trilogy, have found lumps of autobiography sticking up from the tale. That isn't as simple as it may look, and I'll come to it in time. I'm reminded that elements of my life may be traced through my fiction—more of them than may be readily apparent. I hope I don't embarrass myself or the reader too much by owning up to them. Some are trivial: in my early work I was wont to lend characters the names of friends but not usually their characteristics. However, soon enough I took to incorporating more substantial material, often because it was to some extent the source of the tale. Sometimes people were, in the sense that I wrote about them.

Take "Reply Guaranteed." My old friend and agent Kirby McCauley disliked its opening line, but this was a direct quote from my first girlfriend (first, at any rate, apart from infantile infatuations and toddly friendships). It seemed to me to sketch her character, as did the business with the lonely-hearted advert in the tale. My timid relationship with her is also depicted in "The Cellars," based on our exploration of the Liverpool locality that inspired the narrative. I visited her house in Undercliffe Road a couple of times. On one occasion her father advised me to take up dancing and meet a nice girl.

"Concussion" had an odd career. It was based on my next teenage relationship, with a Southend girl I met on a coach back from London. We and her female friend, together with my civil service colleague Jim Smith, went out together for her week on Merseyside. At a necking session she declared me inexperienced, true enough back then, certainly. Learning that I wrote, she asked to be included in a tale, but wasn't altogether pleased to think it would have a horror subject. In fact it didn't; it was untypically romantic, at least for me, although some readers have focused on its paranoia. The first draft used just a general sense of the events of that week and their aftermath. As with several original drafts of the stories in *Demons by Daylight,* I was dissatisfied with it and set it aside. Two years later I wrote complete new versions of them, in its case cleaving much more closely to the actual events and displaying the influence of Alain Resnais. Both approaches much improved the tale.

Between the drafts I'd become briefly engaged, less than halfway through March 1967. I met Rosemary in January, when she was seconded one Saturday to the branch library where I worked. We were parted by her parents in July, but the seeds of devastation were already sown in our relationship, which had been the product of desperation on both sides; the dates betray as much. At the outset we'd discovered we had creativity in common—she was a classical flautist, I was already well in print—but it proved to be far from enough, and eventually we fell to questioning each other's fields with potentially destructive results. I purged myself of grief with a pair of adolescently melodramatic missives to August Derleth and Kirby McCauley, after which I was able to regard the episode as literary material. "The End of a Summer's Day" portrays its subject with little if any exaggeration, and the cave tour was inspired by one we took towards the end of our engagement. "Napier Court" depicts our relationship pretty accurately and yes, I was as insufferable as the protagonist's fiancé; in writing the story, and by no means only that one, I tried to be truthful. The young woman's fate wasn't meant as a literary revenge; in the clumsy first draft this version superseded, the bedridden character was a young man (which made the story's debt to de la Mare's "Out of the Deep" more obvious).

While Rosemary didn't figure in "The Puppets," a reworking of an incident from our time together did. In one of her bids to woo me away from horror she involved me in a concert that included Debussy's *Prélude à l'après-midi d'un faune,* where she was one of the orchestral flautists, though not the soloist. I was delegated to read Mallarmé's poem as an introduction, in French and then in English. I recall stumbling through the original in an intermittent accent of the kind more often heard from foreigners in British comedies—mal armé indeed. My English rendition wasn't much more skilled, and whenever I glanced up from the interminable text I saw the mayor of Hoylake, the venue of the open-air concert, sitting on the front row with his head in his hands. My imagination, if only that, suggests he would have liked to cover his ears. After the concert wine was served, and perhaps this helped him tell me my performance had been a tour de force. He must have been polite to a fault or thoroughly professional—surely not ironic.

"The Other House" derives from nights I slept at Helen Clarke's flat in Liverpool 8. I met Helen while I was working in the music library (where one day Rosemary showed up, apparently unaware that I'd been transferred, but didn't linger). Helen taught English at Quarry Bank High School and later invited me to talk about horror to the sixth form, which proved to include a young Clive Barker. I stayed at her apartment for a week of late-night films (by Melville, Chytilova, Menzel and others) at the Liverpool Everyman, in those days a cinema. I should make clear we were never more than friends.

The Doll Who Ate His Mother was my first completed novel, but that's no excuse for the amount of undigested reportage I included. The meal at the cinema manager's house was unnecessarily closely based on my home life with Jenny, pet rabbit and all, while Claire's nocturnal walk through Newsham Park was simply an account of one I'd taken recently, then a Sunday habit of mine. That location was used to more point in "Mackintosh Willy," itself inspired by aspects of the park (the graffiti in the shelter, the footprints in the concrete). *The Face That Must Die* takes autobiographical material and renders it new, I hope. Alas, my mother lent John Horridge many of her prejudices and mental problems, while acidhead Peter incarnated elements of myself I hoped to leave behind. Indeed, as I wrote one chapter, the aftereffects of a nightmare acid flashback brought my handwriting to unwelcome life.

"The Chimney" retrospectively disconcerted me with its truth to my experience. While writing it I'd thought of it as an invention, since my own Christmases had been magical. Not until I'd read it to guests at Jack Sullivan's apartment in New York years later did I see it had its roots in the only Yuletide terror I'd encountered, when my mother used to send me up to my unseen father's room to knock and invite him down for dinner, though my parents had been estranged since not long after I was born. No wonder (you might think, and I did) that in "The Chimney" the boy's fears transform his father into a festive monster. I'd forgotten this annual dread for most of a decade, a mental quirk that convinces me the vagaries of recall that are central to my novel *Somebody's Voice* are entirely realistic (as does my memory of the violent confrontation that broke up the marriage when I was three, an incident that slipped my mind for decades). R. B. Russell's recent biography of Robert Aickman demonstrates just how unreliable an autobiography (the two volumes Robert wrote) can be and still achieve publication, which is equally relevant to my novel.

"Where the Heart Is" was the product of a creative coincidence. My tales have benefited from many over the years. Kathryn Cramer asked me to write a story for a anthology on the theme of architecture that was in some sense central to the theme. When she sent a letter to potential contributors I was disconcerted to see earlier stories of mine cited as examples—it felt as though I was being asked to replicate myself. Synchronicity came to my aid. As I searched for a suitable idea, Jenny and I and the children moved house. Since we hadn't yet sold our old home, just a walk away at 16 Haydock Road in Wallasey, I visited it daily to see all was well. In time these visits suggested the story I gave Kathryn, though I didn't incorporate the oddest development. When a neighbour told me she'd seen people taking items from the property I reported this to the police, only to be treated like a malefactor by the officer who took me into an interview room. Come to think, when the house where we now live was burgled not long after, an equally unsmiling representative of the law took my fingerprints. Might I have looked too hippyish for the police? Perhaps I ought to thank them for providing potential literary material.

"All for Sale" conflates a couple of incidents. One morning we awoke in our Turkish holiday resort hotel to find a market had appeared overnight in the street outside. More personally, I was appraising videorecorders in a shop on Tottenham

Court Road when the swarthy proprietor approached me to palpate my rather less than masculine breasts and announce "You are nice." My Panther editor Nick Austin was outraged when I recounted the event over a Greek lunch at the Lord Byron, but recollection in tranquillity (if I may quote) let me regard it as an inspiration.

At the turn of the century I began to feel financially insecure, perhaps as a result of the apparent temporary unpopularity of horror fiction. When I learned that the Borders bookshop chain was about to open a local branch, I went to work there. Jenny returned to teaching fulltime, not the first occasion we depended on her—we had for the first five years of my bid to make a living as a writer. The bookshop management arranged my hours so that I could write every day. but I really needed to devote my time to writing, and so I left the shop after six months. I thought it might give me a short story, but when I set about developing the experiences I'd taken home they attracted enough material for a novel. Thus *The Overnight* came into being, even though I hadn't been involved in the titular activity.

And so we come to *The Searching Dead*. Some reviewers have interpreted it as autobiographical, but the elements they've identified tend to be reinvented or even simply made up. While I attended a Catholic grammar school in Liverpool like Dominic, although some years later, his has virtually no teachers in common with mine apart from the drunken Latin master—Harty was the real man's name. (My friend Errol Undercliffe incorporated some of my educational experiences in his tale "The Interloper." After his death the actual maths master Robinson was said to have had a great sense of humour. I must have missed the joke involved in punching a boy in the kidneys for getting an answer wrong and slapping another across the face. I don't believe in writing fiction as revenge, and Undercliffe took none on my behalf, unless you regard accurate depiction as payback.) On the other hand, many of the details of fifties Liverpool are drawn from my life—as many as I could recall and integrate—and the encounter with the dentist happened pretty well as described. As I recall his name was Guthrie-Uchtowski. Perhaps some Polish experience of his had left him with a taste for drilling without administering an anaesthetic. He was a Catholic, and along with the behaviour of the worst staff at my school, his attitude convinced me that religion could do without me.

I was writing about old age long before it caught up with me, and I don't think my depictions have changed much, although the experience has provided new material. One case, although I doubt it's obvious, is "The Operated." Recently I underwent cataract surgery on both eyes, the aftermath of which threw my writing schedule out by several months but was certainly beneficial. It's common these days to declare how much less nightmarish the operation is than one's apprehension suggested, but I couldn't help imagining a situation where it proved to be so hideous that its victims lied about it to wish the same horrors on others as the only consolation. Such a story would have been unforgivably irresponsible, and so I invented an operation for the tale. What experiences may be yet to come? My imagination remains alert, and I can only hope senility doesn't rob me of technique, even if I forget to put in the occasional or even the odd punctuation mark

Kreegah Bundolo!

Darrell Schweitzer

WILL MURRAY. *King Kong vs. Tarzan*. Illustrated by Joe DeVito. n.p.: Altus Press, 2016. 465 pp. $24.95 tpb. ISBN 9781618272812.

This is something of a follow-up to my report on Pulpfest in *Dead Reckonings* 30. I mentioned that Will Murray (who has also written Lovecraftian fiction) is virtually a one-man pulp fiction industry, who has authored more than seventy books, not the least of which include new and authorized adventures of Doc Savage, The Shadow, Tarzan of the Apes, and the recent crossover, *John Carter, Conqueror of Mars*. He is an all-purpose pulpster. If anybody needed new adventures of G-8 and His Battle Aces or Operator 5, Murray is the writer to do it.

I was surprised to learn (from Wikipedia) that a King Kong vs. Tarzan movie was actually contemplated by Merian C. Cooper in the 1930s, but there were problems clearing the rights. Now the rights have been cleared and we have a 400+-page novel, in which the ape-man battles the biggest ape of them all for mastery of the African jungle.

How Kong got to the African jungle is much of the story. The original film, the 1933 novelization, and subsequent re-makes all skip over the details of how showman Carl Denham actually got Kong from Skull Island (which is somewhere in the eastern Indian Ocean) to New York. Therein lies much of the tale. How *do* you keep a fantastically strong, thirty-foot gorilla alive in the hold of a tramp freighter for weeks or even months? The answer is that he is kept sedated the whole time, but slowly fed, and aided by the herbal lore of an old woman from Skull Island who has been his priestess ever since he was a wee ten-foot gorilla. But even this barely works, and when the ship can't go through the Suez Canal (due to the impossibility of explaining Kong to customs officials) and must sail around Africa, first putting in for supplies and fresh water on the coast of Kenya, Kong wakes up, escapes, and wreaks havoc in a jungle not at all like what he is used to. (Kong prefers a diet of dinosaurs. The best he can do is devour alligators by the handful and, at one point, a hippopotamus.) This is of course not the real Africa, for all it may have real places (Mombasa is mentioned) on the coast. It is Tarzan's Africa, which is as imaginary as Barsoom, containing no real cultures (Murray skirts around the issue of racism very easily; there are no native Africans in the story until the epilogue, where we glimpse a few Waziri at Tarzan's estate), and inhabited by the "anthropoid apes" (the ones who raised Tarzan) of a species unknown to science. The ape-man of course is lord over all he surveys, able to speak to various species of animals in their own languages, and command them. But his realm is threatened, not merely by the physical damage that Kong does, but because some of the apes get it into their heads that Tarzan is no longer master; Kong is their new god. A showdown is inevitable.

Murray manages to keep the voyage and the initial adventures interesting, in fact quite entertaining. This is a real page-turner, even if the reader is left waiting, and waiting, for Tarzan to show up. The ape-man is first mentioned as a rumor on page 122. On page 170 (chapter 25) we are given the point of view of Nkima, a monkey in Tarzan's employ. Tarzan himself does not actually appear until page 262. Meanwhile the narrative has been brisk and efficient. The characterizations are good, as far as they go. First Mate Driscoll romances Ann Darrow. Captain Englehorn is a crusty old salt, but sensible and fair. Old Penjaga, the witch woman from Skull Island, disapproves of the whole blasphemous affair, but still faithfully serves Kong. Carl Denham, the showman, is very close to being a sociopath, unscrupulous, egotistical, motivated entirely by avarice, utterly indifferent to the various people who lose their lives in the course of his pet project, but, like many sociopaths, very persuasive. ("I am glad you agree with me that Carl Denham is an asshole," I remarked to Murray at Pulpfest. He merely replied that he had to follow the original novelization.)

Kong heads for Mount Kilimanjaro, intending to rule this new land from a height, as he did Skull Island. How he is lured back to the coast and recaptured with the aid of Tarzan, four elephants, and the Golden Lion, makes for a thrilling, if somewhat overly adjectival narrative. One does notice that Murray writes best when there is a lot of dialogue and things are moving along briskly. When he gets into the thunderous battle between ape and ape-man, he tends to lay on phrases like "the apish ogre" and "the huge ape-thing" (in the same sentence), followed by "the bristling black behemoth," "the gargantuan anthropoid," "the Cyclopean creature," "the beast god," "the prehistoric gorilla," etc. etc. a bit too thickly. None of this is necessary because by this point we already know who and what Kong is, what he looks like and what he is capable of. Surely one of the tricks of good action writing is to make such descriptions as spare as possible once things get going furiously, because all they do is remind the reader of what the reader already knows. The editor in me wanted to reach for the blue pencil, but I don't deface books, so instead I found myself simply skimming over the redundant verbiage. It's such a grand story that you can do that.

Of course, the plot has to dovetail back into the continuity of the movie and original novelization. Tarzan, who has come to respect Kong, wants him to be returned to Skull Island, but through the treachery of Carl Denham Kong ends up in New York. Tarzan, back on his estate in Africa, reads of the giant ape's fate in a newspaper. You can be certain that if Tarzan and Denham ever meet again, the encounter will be short, and fatal for Denham.

This book is in its own way, great stuff, filled with the sort of spectacle that would work well on the big screen. Maybe one day Merian C. Cooper will get his wish . . .

Richard L. Tierney: A Brief Memoir

Leigh Blackmore

I never met Dick "Eldritchard" Tierney in person. I had long been a fan of his work, dating from the late 1970s when I first read his work in American fanzines and semiprozines including *Nyctalops, The Arkham Collector, Eldritch Tales, Etchings and Odysseys,* and *Whispers.* Starting with *The Winds of Zarr* (1975), I began to read his fiction as well. As an Arkham House devotee and weird poetry enthusiast, I devoured his *Collected Poems* (1981).

It was not until the 2000s, when my close friend Charles Danny Lovecraft, publisher at Sydney's P'rea Press, began to contact Dick Tierney regularly by email, that I began to do the same. I gradually grew closer to Eldritchard. His emails were infrequent, since he had no email access at his home and could only send messages from the PC at his local library in Mason City, Iowa, near his birthplace in Spencer, Iowa.

Eventually, in 2009, I wrote to him, enclosing some blank book labels, with a request that he sign them and return them to me so I could affix them in my copies of the many books of his now in my collection—the Red Sonja novels he co-authored with David C Smith, plus *For the Witch of the Mists;* his Cthulhu Mythos novel *The House of the Toad;* his Simon of Gitta volumes *The Scroll of Thoth* and *The Drums of Chaos,* and other odd volumes such as his poetry chapbook *The Blob That Gobbled Adul and Others* and his Robert E. Howard completions. Dick kindly signed the labels and duly returned them, with the one and only letter in his own handwriting that I ever received from him. His letter contained some pithy memories of his five-months' spell in 1964 visiting Lovecraftian sites in and around in Providence, R.I., while he completed a graduate course in entomology at the University of Massachusetts in Amherst. His missive ended with the sharply iconoclastic sentiment: "I think we Lovecraftians are always in the minority, 'Down Under' or not. Maybe it's 'cause we sense that the human race isn't such hot shit on the cosmic scale & that outlook is never going to be popular.—Al-hamdu Tsatgg-ullah, Dick."

In 2010, Charles Danny Lovecraft issued the new collected poems of "Eldritchard" (covering the years 1982–2010) as *Savage Menace and Other Poems of Horror* (Sydney: Pre'a Press) in hardcover (limited edition) and paperback. Dick was soon thereafter nominated for Grandmaster of the Science Fiction Poetry Association.

There followed more email correspondence. In 2011, I had the honour of editing *Midnight Echo* magazine No. 5 for the Australian Horror Writers Association, of which I was then president. I devoted considerable space in the issue to weird verse as well as to weird fiction, and invited Dick Tierney to collaborate with me on a poem for which I outlined the concept and the rhyme scheme. We wrote stanzas in turn, and the result, "Twilight of the Mage" (a stylistic tribute to our inescapable mutual poetic influence, Clark Ashton Smith), is included here in tribute. I am privileged to have collaborated with one of the great weird writers of twentieth century—an experience for which I am both humbled and proud.

Danny and I continued to maintain regular contact with Dick over the next decade. After his deteriorating health necessitated his transfer to a nursing home, we were able to speak to him regularly by phone, bringing both Danny and me into even greater contact and intimacy (though from an international distance) with the Great Old One. Dick was mentally acute to the end, always full of good humor, willing to discuss his work, self-deprecating, happy to discuss his friends, his influences, his love of the golden age of weird writing, and (despite his reputation as a fierce nihilist and atheist) ever a kindly soul to deal with in person.

I'll remember Dick Tierney primarily as a superb weird poet, though his essays and fiction will also stand the test of time, and he was a sculptor to boot and no mean artist. Some of the poems that appeared in *Collected Poems: Nightmares and Visions* were printed in a prestigious two-page spread in the May 1982 issue of *Twilight Zone* magazine. Let us remind ourselves how few poets have such an honor accorded them in a newsstand-distributed magazine.

That first collection of scintillating weird verse (we shall disregard the ill-fated *Dreams and Damnations* of slightly earlier date) received a glowing, adulatory three-page review in the pages of *Nyctalops* No. 18 (1983) by weird poetry specialist Steve Eng. Eng pointed out, among other virtues of Tierney's verse, his exceptional and genuine sense of place; his subtlety and use of quiet endings in his sonnets rather than the declamatory, and somewhat clichéd, melodramatic final couplet employed by many weird sonneteers; Tierney's range of effects, from chilling horror to eerie strangeness to musicality and delicacy at times, along with the ability to write with the energy and verve of a Robert E. Howard where appropriate. Eng goes so far (and I believe he is not mistaken) as to place certain of Tierney's verses on the same plane as work by Wilde, Ernest Dowson, and Thomas Burnett Swann. Nor should it be forgotten that Tierney is one of a select group of American poets who have translated some Baudelaire into English (among them Clark Ashton Smith, Edna St. Vincent Millay, and George Dillon), and that some of his translations bid fair to be among the most memorable of those attempted in our tongue. It is to be regretted that he never completed a full translation of *Les Fleurs du mal*.

Eng wrote at the time that "Tierney hopefully will . . . not 'outgrow' poetry, for he has much more and much else to give." This was amply proven in 2010 with the publication of *Savage Menace and Other Poems of Horror*. P'rea Press currently has in preparation a much-expanded edition of *Savage Menace,* including all Tierney's verses written between 2010 and his death on February 1, 2022, together with some overlooked and previously uncollected gems. I have contributed a longer appreciation of "Eldritchard" there than the brief space here in *Dead Reckonings* permits. And with the new editions of *Sorcery against Caesar* and *The Drums of Chaos* from Pickman's Press (out now), there is plenty of Richard L. Tierney around to be savored and enjoyed to the full.

Twilight of the Mage

Leigh Blackmore and Richard L. Tierney

From shadow-sunken distant spheres
Where leaden skies o'ershadow strands
Far-strewn with wrack and witch-wrought spells
And brakes of deep funereal trees—
Command your gramarye of fears
Whose demoniac memory brands
Your magic; locked in haunted cells
Grim ghouls, capricious, seek to please.

This world is waning down to doom;
The darkness mounts, the red sun fades.
Even those ghouls peer eerily
At signs that the expanding sun
Is dimming to a crimson gloom.
The winds blow chill oe'r lakes and glades
And streams that once flowed cheerily—
All frozen now, their courses run.

The ruined ramparts of your tower
Beneath unshapen worlds rise drear.
Fretful, you roam the spectred halls
Of veined adamantine stone
Where braziers flame, illume the power
Of faded spells sundered by fear.
Fast-gyved by fate, restriction galls
Your being—assailed and alone.

And now, your gramarye in this
Grim age of hard technology
Seems not to pow'r your howled commands
But, unresponsive to your pleas
To beneficial sprites of bliss,
A cloud descends most balefully,

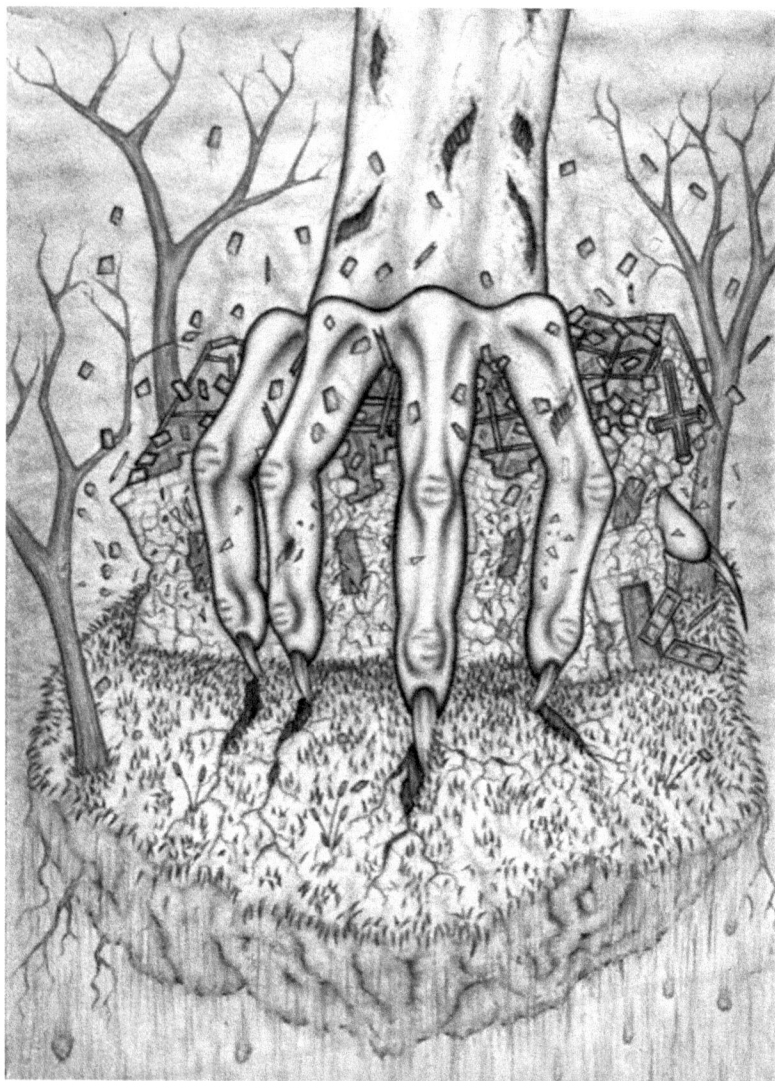

Grip of God *by Shane K. Ryan*

Dead Reckonings

Stifling your frantic, crazed demands
That once fulfilled your will with ease.

The world is waning down to doom;
The red sun fades, the darkness mounts,
Casting its pall of purpling shades—
Ill-omened all your desperate spells.
Your pallid pride and foul perfume,
Resistant though your fate surmounts
All efforts to o'ercome; life fades—
Succumb now to thy nether hells.

Wollongong and Mason City, Iowa, June–August 2010.

The Brief Biblio-Historiography of a Consequential Scribbler

Edward Guimont

S. T. JOSHI. *The Recognition of H. P. Lovecraft: His Rise from Obscurity to World Renown*. New York: Hippocampus Press, 2021. 340 pp. $25.00 softcover. ISBN 9781614983453 (paperback). ISBN 9781614983460 (ebook).

It was in the summer of 1996 when, as a child, I accompanied my parents to a bluegrass festival in upstate New York. Wandering the various vendors, I came across one selling a pin featuring a scowling cephalopod with the caption, "Smile—Cthulhu Loathes You!" Asking the vendor what this was, I was told that it was an alien from a book. Later that year I purchased a hardcover copy of *Barlowe's Guide to Extraterrestrials,* still one of my favorite science fiction reference books. There, in between the illustrations of aliens from such cherished books as *Dune* and *Ringworld,* was a depiction of a barrel-chested creature with membraneous wings. The text identified this as an "Old One" from the works of an author I was unfamiliar with named H. P. Lovecraft (Barlowe, Summers, and Meacham 68–69).

It was only years later that I would put the two together. How did it get to the fact that, almost sixty years after the (literal) death of the author, my first exposure to Lovecraft was not from his writings but from a pin and an art book on classic sci-fi aliens? As it would happen, the same year of my exposure to Lovecraft, S. T. Joshi published two books on him, *H. P. Lovecraft: A Life* and *A Subtler Magick* (Joshi 237–39). These were important works in both the biographical scholarship of Lovecraft and the output of Joshi—and in both cases, are vital links in the chain that leads to *The Recognition of H. P. Lovecraft.*

Joshi and his seminal role in the field of Lovecraftian scholarship needs no introduction for the readership of *Dead Reckon-*

ings. That Joshi has been so central to Lovecraftian scholarship for so long is evident from the fact that *The Recognition of H. P. Lovecraft* shares its name and theme with a five-page manuscript on the topic Joshi co-authored in 1978 (Joshi and Michaud 2–7). The span of forty-three years has swelled that fanzine article to a 340-page manuscript from a publisher devoted almost entirely to Lovecraft's work, in which Joshi is a central figure. On his blog, Joshi is entirely correct, and perhaps even understating things, when he describes *The Recognition of H. P. Lovecraft* as "a pretty significant title in terms of my coverage of both the dissemination of Lovecraft's work worldwide and the criticism of his life, work, and thought over the decades." Over the course of nine chapters Joshi explores how Lovecraft was perceived by others, both within and outside the realm of genre authors and fans, and how various tropes about the author and his work developed, expanded, and were challenged, as the popularity of Lovecraft's work grew.

The first two chapters, "Beginnings (1905–1922)" and "The Pulp Era (1923–1937)," document the coverage of Lovecraft during his lifetime. Joshi argues that some of the earliest criticism of Lovecraft's fiction in the amateur press probably helped shape Lovecraft's own worldview on the nature of weird fiction and of the audience that an author should write for. Ironically, these attitudes, once solidified and mixed with Lovecraft's lack of belief in his tales and lack of reception to editorial suggestion, may have cost him potential publishing deals with Simon & Schuster and Knopf during his lifetime. However, after Lovecraft became more established, criticism of his work via letters to "The Eyrie" column of *Weird Tales* was often a gateway to the critic moving to authorship themselves. Further, from the late 1920s onward, Lovecraft was discussed—albeit not always positively—by a wider range of literary figures and publications than might be expected. Overall, I found these first two chapters to be the most interesting, giving a glimpse into how one might have first been introduced to Lovecraft during his lifetime.

If the first two chapters were the most interesting to me, the third, "Arkham House: The Early Years (1937–1945)," I found to be the book's strongest intervention into Lovecraftian historiography. Even those who disapprove of August Derleth's writing style, personality, or understanding of Lovecraft and his themes will generally grant that it was only due to Derleth's ironclad stewardship of Lovecraft's corpus through Arkham House for thirty years that Lovecraft was remembered at all. Instead, Joshi illustrates that Derleth's stubbornness, lack of business sense, and unwillingness to cede any control over the Lovecraft estate he had seized severely delayed and limited the scope of the early Arkham House publications. Indeed, Arkham House itself only emerged due to the fact that Derleth was unwilling to cut down on the stories he wanted to include in *The Outsider and Others;* had he relented, it could well have been published by a larger, more established press like Simon & Schuster or Scribner's. Through examinations of these and other publishing mishaps, Joshi shows that far from Derleth being the savior of Lovecraft's memory, "Lovecraft's popular and critical acclaim may have been delayed or derailed because of these fateful decisions." For critics of Derleth, this chapter will provide powerful ammunition against his strongest bulwark.

In the fourth chapter, "The Beginnings of Worldwide Dissemination (1946–1959)," Joshi charts how Lovecraft's recognition continued to rise until 1945, an "annus horribilis" symbolized by a hostile review by the *New Yorker* critic Edmund Wilson, leading to a period of decline in Lovecraftian scholarship and review. However, even such an impactful negative review is illustrative in that Wilson still grants some bits of praise to Lovecraft as both a man and author, including making the prescient connection of "The Colour out of Space" to the atomic bomb, less than four months after Hiroshima—and it should be noted that the reception of that tale in its native *Amazing Stories* is analyzed for the first time in this volume.

Joshi argues that the decline of Lovecraft's presence among established critics and press is, again, largely due to Derleth's reaction to Wilson and other reviewers, not the reviewers themselves. But he also contrasts this with the fact that Lovecraft was still widely read by fans, including new ones, in this period. What is more, fandom started to divide into familiar camps at this point, including those devoted to categorizing the emergent "Cthulhu Mythos" and those now hostile to either Lovecraft's style or his "cult," positions still familiar among fans eighty years later. But of most interest in this chapter are the first discussions of Lovecraft reprints abroad, first in Britain and then translations in continental Europe. Throughout the book, Joshi traces the early spread of Lovecraft into foreign languages (including surprisingly early appearances in communist bloc countries); this was not only another highlight for me (and an impressive piece of historical detective work) but a fertile field for scholars of those national literatures to explore deeper.

The exploration of Lovecraft's translations continues in chapter five, "Paperbacks and Movies (1960–1971)," along with the resumption of Lovecraft's popularity in the U.S. in that decade, exhibited by the beginnings of the venerable genre of "shlocky loose Lovecraftian film adaptation." The decade also saw the arrival of such core pastiche authors as Lin Carter and Ramsey Campbell, but most significantly for scholarship, it saw the start of Arkham House's publication of the *Selected Letters*. The *Selected Letters* project would outlast its initiator, as Derleth died in 1971, leading to chapter six, "The Revival of Scholarship (1971–1979)." The end of Derleth's litigious control of Lovecraft's legacy led to a flowering of new scholarship and pastiche alike, symbolically inaugurated by Richard L. Tierney's article "The Derleth Mythos," arguably the most significant single page of Lovecraft scholarship (Tierney 53). The key figure in this emerging renaissance of scholarship was Dirk Mosig, who served as a mentor to figures like Peter Cannon and Joshi himself, who enters the book as a subject here.

And it is here where the secondary value of the book comes in: the final few chapters serve almost as a mini-biography of Joshi, at least in his role as a Lovecraftian scholar. This is not in any way meant to portray Joshi as hubristic or myopic in writing himself into the historical narrative; how could he not include himself in a work on the reception, discussion, criticism, and scholarship of Lovecraft? Anyone covering this topic would be bound to make Joshi at least one of a few central figures of the last few decades. In this way, while *Recognition* is first and foremost a study of Lovecraftian scholarship and critique as well as how his popular appeal evolved, the final third also works as a study of Joshi's contributions to that field. For its part, the biographical element is aided by the fact that Joshi's voice and personality come across a bit less filtered in *Recognition* than some of his prior academic works of the last thirty years, giving it the feel of a more informal and intimate read, even in the areas where Joshi is completely absent.

As such, Joshi's work is increasingly featured in chapters seven and eight, "Looking toward the Centennial (1980–1990)" and "The Road to Canonisation (1991–2005)," but it is hardly the only focus. Names still active in the field, like Will Murray and Jason Colavito, as well as institutions like Hippocampus Press and NecronomiCon, start to appear at this point, as Lovecraft begins to spread through popular culture, fueled by the crystallization of the "Cthulhu Mythos" as not only a setting, but one with an appeal almost separate from Lovecraft, and in some cases, his work itself. As much of this period will be fresher in most readers' minds, I will not go into as in-depth a summary; suffice it to say that Joshi's attempt to chart Lovecraft's reception in wider pop culture is brave, but not entirely comprehensive. This is no fault of his own, but rather a testament to just how widespread Lovecraft's legacy had become by the twenty-first century, and Joshi still is able to effectively chart the miraculous interventions on the path to canonization.

Given the escalating cultural spread of Lovecraft, no longer merely in genre circles, it makes sense that the ninth and final chapter, "Dissemination and Controversy (2006–2020)," is the longest. It is also probably the most controversial, far more so than the earlier criticisms of Derleth, if for no other reason than the controversy in question is one that still rages, and in which Joshi has been a central figure. This is, of course, the now decade-old debate over Lovecraft's racism, which Joshi charts as being inaugurated by a 2013 blog post of the author P. Djèlí Clark.[1] Clark's criticism sparked a movement whose peak was the 2015 decision to replace the bust of

---

1. For full disclosure, in graduate school, Clark was one of my professors, and for a time my neighbor. However, we never discussed Lovecraft.

Lovecraft from the award statuette of the World Fantasy Convention, an organization whose inaugural 1975 meeting was essentially a commemoration of Lovecraft.

The division of the community over the issue has become so bitter and entrenched that Joshi is unlikely to make any converts to his position. However, his coverage of the drama gives him the space to articulate the core element of his position, one whose nuance is not always appreciated when Joshi's position is stated by those on the side of Clark and his successors: "One of the most galling features of the whole controversy is the alacrity in which certain figures who have benefited from Lovecraft's popularity—and the popularity of weird fiction that he has helped to engender—are prepared to kick Lovecraft posthumously while continuing to profit from their own Lovecraftian writings." And as Joshi notes, many of the present controversies over Lovecraft are not new. The same with the stereotypes of him and his fans—including complaints about oversaturation and annoying fandom—many of which emerged in the first years after Lovecraft's death. within years of his death.

However, it should be noted that the discussion of the racism issue is at the very end of the last chapter of the book. The preceding bulk of the ninth chapter is an exploration of the various pastiches, scholarly work,[2] comics, movies, and games which have exploded in the past fifteen years. And, to draw it full circle, it includes references to such merchandise as Cthulhu for President stickers and Lovecraftian Christmas ornaments. If anything, the only notable thing about me encountering a Cthulhu pin in 1996 was that the vendor was on the cutting edge of Lovecraftian merchandising.

For those interested in Lovecraftian scholarship, a work by Joshi needs no hyping. But even for someone like me, who has dug fairly deep into the topic of the spread of criticism and commentary on Lovecraft, *Recognition* only made me realize how shallowly I had scratched the surface. In contrast, while some very basic knowledge of Lovecraft and his works

2. As another point of full disclosure, this includes a positive comment about one of my own articles (Guimont 52-69).

are necessary, this is not an inscrutable grimoire for a hypothetical new initiate into the Cult of Lovecraft. For all its deep dives (annotated and cited) into occasionally obscure appearances of Lovecraft in media, there is no difficulty in following the narrative. Events in his life are (for the most part) at least briefly explained; figures are introduced when they appear on the scene; and context is provided for actions taken (or not). Given the lack of publication in his own lifetime, one wonders what Lovecraft would make of this book—although one suspects he might be self-deprecating enough to protest that a "nonentity" like himself was undeserving of both the widespread dissemination, and such an impressive piece of research charting it. To anyone who would consider buying this book, however—we all know the truth.

Works Cited

Barlowe, Wayne Douglas; Summers, Ian; and Meacham, Beth. *Barlowe's Guide to Extraterrestrials*. 1979. New York: Workman Publishing, 1987.

Guimont, Edward. "At the Mountains of Mars: Viewing the Red Planet through a Lovecraftian Lens." In *Lovecraftian Proceedings No. 3,* ed. Dennis P. Quinn. New York: Hippocampus Press, 2019. 52–69.

Joshi, S. T., and Marc A. Michaud. "The Recognition of H. P. Lovecraft." *Lovecraftian Ramblings* No. 8 (1978): 2–7.

Tierney, Richard L. "The Derleth Mythos." In *HPL,* ed. Meade Frierson and Penny Frierson. Birmingham, AL: Meade & Penny Frierson, 1972. 53.

Sprawling, Taxing, Rewarding

Géza A. G. Reilly

WILLIAM BROWN and DAVID H. FLEMING. *The Squid Cinema from Hell:* Kinoteuthis Infernalis *and the Emergence of Chthulumedia*. Edinburgh: Edinburgh University Press, 2020. 328 pp. $33.95 tpb. ISBN: 9781474463737.

The Squid Cinema from Hell is a difficult book. It is also, I think, a good book, and I recommend it, but that recommendation comes with caveats for a general audience. *The Squid Cinema from Hell* is an academic work through and through, and to get the most out of it, the reader will have to come to the text with a solid grounding in media studies, bioethics, and modern philosophy–or be willing to do at least some ancillary reading at the same time. Authors William Brown and David H. Fleming have given us an insightful and provocative text, but I cannot comfortably say that it is for everyone.

The basic argument in *The Squid Cinema from Hell* is that we as a species are on the cusp of leaving the anthropocene (the geological period in which human civilization has been the dominant influence upon the planet) and entering into the chthulucene (when the media/the cephalopod is the dominant influence upon the planet) due at least in part to the advent of digital media (or "Chthulumedia"). The term "chthulucene" comes from Donna J. Haraway, perhaps most famous for her stunning essay "The Cyborg Manifesto" (*Socialist Review,* 1985), and stems from "chthonic" rather than the "Cthulhu" of Lovecraft fame. However, Brown and Fleming play with the confusion between the two in this overtly and intentionally sprawling, soft book.

In a variety of ways, *The Squid Cinema from Hell* makes the case that the emergence of digital media allows us to understand the points of similarity—even commonality—with cephalopods. By doing so, the text wants the reader to discover the ways in which "the barriers, divisions, borders, and separations between things are an anthropocentric conceit—albeit one that is perhaps necessary for the lifestyle to which many humans have become accustomed." They are certainly not alone in their pinpointing cephalopods as comparable to, compatible with, or the same as humanity. Authors such as Gilles Deleuze and Félix Guattari are drawn on repeatedly, and works such as Vilém Flusser's excellent *Vampyroteuthis Infernalis: A Treatise with a Report* are referenced in order to interrogate the ways in which human preoccupations with our own senses blind us to other, possibly richer, ways of living (embedded) within the world. As the authors put it, "the cephalopod is perhaps the very meta-metaphor that connotes the truth of metaphoricity, not just in the sense that we live by metaphors, but also in the sense that metaphors themselves connote a world of connection and non-differentiation." Indeed, the authors theorize that cephalopods/digital media/Chthulumedia might very well be "hypercryptids" that, borrowing from Timothy Morton's definition of "hyperobjects," are "complex meshes of *interobjectivity*, wherein 'nothing is ever experienced directly, but only as mediated through other entities in some shared sensual space'" and which might be echoing through everything forwards and backwards in time.

Stirring stuff! In their pursuits, Brown and Fleming move through everything from media archaeology to 4DX cinema to Scarlett Johansson (and the division between ScarJo, CharJo, and "{Schar-J0}") to Denis Villeneuve's *Arrival* to hentai to Lovecraft's Cthulhu and more. Indeed, Cthulhu itself is used as an example of theoretical superpositions ("whereby a phenomenon can be in two different, supposedly contradictory positions at once," drawing in part on Graham Harmon's *Weird Realism: Lovecraft and Philosophy*), denoting two potential outcomes of Chthulumedia moving us into the chthulucene. One is the result of Chthulumedia tempting us into a "technologized patriarchy" that is anti-death and obsessed with the immortality of the image. This is the rule of corporations and capitalism taken beyond the bounds of Fredric Jameson's late stage and right into a nightmare of personal, class, and societal rigidity (paradoxically, the cephalopodic media perverted into preserving solid-boned structures of never-ending youth and beauty). The other is one in which we have learned to embrace death and the permeability of ourselves and our bodies as subjects, becoming more open to the "soft" and whole-bodied sensory experience of the world. This latter option is what Brown and Fleming refer to as the humiliation of the human and is the preferable of the two ways we can go ("The chthulucene, then, involves humiliation before planetary powers and a dark universe that we do not/cannot understand [. . .] the chthulucene may well involve a renewed understanding of orgasm, as we learn to take joy in our bodily existence with the world–with the tentacles of the cephalopod, or of Cthulhu, thus suggesting an ec-static move away from the stasis of perpetual life").

So it is worth wondering whether or not *The Squid Cinema from Hell* presents a convincing argument. Unfortunately, the text is a collection of complex assertions set loose to sprawl in the marketplace, and whether the authors' arguments are persuasive is something that can be determined only by the individual reader. This is not to say that I distrust what Brown and Fleming have argued; on the level of bioethics, media studies, and philosophy, I certainly think they have made a (perhaps ironically) solid case for what they have set out to investigate. At the same time, however, I did leave *The Squid Cinema from Hell* with certain questions. I was left wondering, for example, what precisely is the point of departure from non-Chthulumedia into Chthulumedia proper. Certainly, Brown and Fleming repeatedly stress the ways in which books themselves are tied into their meta-metaphor of the cephalopod (by ink), so why are they not just as vitally a part of Chthulumedia as 4DX theaters, Instagram, or smartphones? Why did their emergence not trigger the twilight of the anthropocene and the advent of the chthulucene?

These are minor matters, however. *The Squid Cinema from Hell* is a sprawling, insightful, and really quite difficult set of commentaries on new ways of seeing, thinking, and conceptualizing ourselves, our products, and the world around us. It does sound alarm bells, yes, but not in the sense of any screed or manifesto. Instead, it encourages us to avoid putting ourselves on a pedestal—individually or collectively—and to understand how current cultural preoccupations might just lead us merrily into disaster (after all, as S. T. Joshi and others have pointed out, there is no reason to think that Cthulhu cultists are right in their beliefs, let alone in their expectations of rewards bestowed upon them by their purported gods). Ultimately, I recommend *The Squid Cinema from Hell* to those who are interested in struggling with difficult ideas about how we might know and understand the world differently. However, new ideas can come with associated pain—adjustment to alien, cephalopodic ways of experience are hard for just about anyone. Willing readers will need to grapple (softly, even tenderly) with almost every page of this dense, taxing, and rewarding text.

Welcome Horrors from Down Under

Leigh Blackmore

DAVID KURARIA. *Bedding the Lamia: Tropical Horrors.* Gold Coast, Australia: IFGW Publishing International, 2021. 202 pp. RRP: UK £11.99, AU $20.95, US $14.99, EU €12.99 tpb. ISBN 9781922556240.

First, let's clear up one thing, in relation to the book's title. Rather akin to the famous "curious incident of the dog in the night-time" in the Sherlock Holmes story "Silver Blaze," in which the curious incident was that "the dog did nothing in the night-time," there is no lamia in this book. Great title, though! *Bedding the Lamia* is Kuraria's first collection. It contains four stories, two previously published in magazines. Two of the four tales are short stories, while the others are novellas, one of which ("The Absurd Quest of Thomas Wu") occupies more than half the book's length.

The collection opens strongly with the excellent longish tale "The Gods of Mwaia," starting in Honiara. Kuraria mixes invented locales and epigrams from non-existent books with actual locales and backgrounds using the time-honored technique Lovecraft dubbed "pseudo-authentication." "Kiwi" man Alan O'Connor, who has the rare condition of argyria, a blue-gray silvering of the skin, accompanies his Melanesian friend Renai (from the island of "Mwaia"), a farmer seeking land rights from a dominant tribe on the island; Tatau, a female doctor; and La'akwai, a guy who constantly smokes weed, on a trip to meet the upland Kwaio people of the island. The Kwaio keep themselves in isolation from all other members of society. Their ways are of magic and sorcery. The Honiara party bear gifts of persuasion to the Kwaio through the tropical foliage, but then stumble across a sacred site of weathered standing stones covered in petroglyphs and, as it turns out, hallucinogenic moss. What follows is classic Kuraria, as the frightful gods of the Kwaio make themselves known. This is a tightly plotted and written story, with some graphic scenes but much of the horror suggested and some aspects left ambiguous to the end. It is bound to satisfy anyone with a thirst for exotic horror.

Set in Sydney's Central Business Distrct, "And He Shall Suffer for His Art," is a concise and cutting tale about the reclusive Mack, an artist experimenting with narcotics, painting with his own blood and obscure occult techniques. Like a perverse variant on Lovecraft's "Pickman's Model," with overtones of David Morrell's "Orange Is for Anguish, Blue for Insanity," but with a definite originality and flavor all its own, this tale packs a wallop, as Mack's friend Rennie catches up with his old mate only to discover how far into delusional weirdness his friend has fallen. A grotesque winner.

"Silent Is the River" takes us to novella form, as a group of holidaymakers travel through the croc-infested waters of the Edward Pellew Islands of the Gulf of Carpentaria in Australia's far North on a boat fatefully named (in jest) the *Mary Celeste*. Jack, Jarra, Fred, Chugger, Dien, and the young Kiwi woman Angie are a motley crew. Kuraria's influence from writers such as William Hope Hodgson, with his ghostly tales of the sea, shows through strongly in places here, with excellent and authentic detail of life aboard ship and technicalities of the vessel, though Kuraria's own clearly extensive research and experience come into play as well. The tale provides convincing and haunting historical background on the area's colonial Chinese, Muslim, Indigenous, and convict past, and the criminal past of North Australia's early settlements.

But as it gradually becomes clear that the secondhand vessel is actually a converted war barge once used to retrieve the corpses of fallen soldiers, the horror mounts and events begin to spiral out of control. What follows, including death by overhanging branch, razor-sharp bollard, and tentacled monstrosities, among others, form an adeptly handled mixture of graphic and visceral episodes. These are interspersed amidst more creeping and suggestive horrors in which the author shows admirable restraint in description, as in the passage where "Dien watched with growing horror the many-armed shadow moving up towards the darkness of the ceiling, where he felt something best not seen waited for him to move." In the denouement, only two of the crew escape alive. Kuraria excels at stories set in obscure and underutilized locales, and this is one of his most effectively conceived and executed stories.

The even longer novella, "The Absurd Quest of Thomas Wu," begins with the titular Wu surviving the Christchurch earthquakes. Inheriting his deceased grandfather's diaries, once again rather like a professorial narrator in a Lovecraft tale (though this character is a timorous and indeed cowardly bookseller, who fails to assist others in the earthquake upheavals), he decides to recreate the old man's equatorial travels. Tom Wu travels from Christchurch via Sydney and Port Moresby, then via Rabaul on East New Britain in the Bismarck Archipelago north of Papua New Guinea, to a tiny Micronesian island, one of the "Tokonu group" beyond Rabaul.

After thirty pages, what seems set up to be another promising tropical horror story veers into fantasy territory, and into an absurd humor I found less entertaining. After checking into a local hotel, Wu wanders the twilight island. From a narrow bridge, he strays across a borderland of some kind and steps into an "otherworld"—a surrealistic hellscape in which he is ordered about by an elephant-eared, demonic minion named Stenching. Purgatoria is filled with red haze and people imprisoned in filth pits. Then Nil, a snouted, fanged, Gorgon-headed creature with a vagina impossible to ignore, appears. She lives in a fissure on a rock-strewn mountain, eats truffles from an earthen bowl, and owns a bound set of official papers. Nil, a dreaded "overseer" creature of this land of Purgatoria, takes control of Tom a while. Wu, captured by the faceless (except for smirking mouths) Nuns of Discord, who bake people in ovens, is rescued by Nil, who seems to have sexual designs on him as she is trying to get pregnant. Tom finds himself dragged along through lava tubes and across plains and valleys toward a place named Agarthi, where he is destined to be brought to a being referred to as *the Foul Flower."* Though Tom suspects he is drugged, dreaming, or possibly having a psychotic episode, Stenching informs Tom his experiences are real. At the Hall of Records are two silly demonic clerks, Fer and Smug, who are featured largely through the rest of the narrative. Purgatoria's native creatures are uniformly ugly, having features such as "tumour sacs" dangling under their throats.

And so it continues. There's a rock band called Vulvathoom with a lead singer named Grimknacker. There are transparent creatures called Oscolids, and we also find a couple of Mythos references. Part 10 has a Kurarian in-joke. Stenching meets his uncle, named Diabolous. Tom Wu undergoes an astounding climactic transformation. The dialogue and situations are, one supposes, blackly comedic—maybe something like Terry Pratchett if he was ordered to write *The Inferno;* but this absurd quest is an acquired taste, and it's one this reviewer was (regrettably) unable to acquire. It will perhaps appeal to readers who appreciate an uneasy parody of Dante that falls somewhere between outright grotesquerie and straight-ahead humour.

Publicity would have us believe that David Kuraria, of Melanesian and Scottish heritage, was born on the island of Ranongga in the Solomon Islands and attended Kingsland Intermediate School in Auckland, New Zealand, before reuniting with his family in the Solomon's capital, Honiara, where he is employed in habitat protection by the Honiara Department of Fisheries. A quick check of the ISFDB database reveals, however, that Kuraria is a *nom de plume* of well-known New Zealand–born Australian horror writer, magazine and anthology editor and artist Bryce Stevens. Stevens has previously published the small-press horror collections *Pale Flesh* (Borderlands Press, 1989), *Skin Tight* (Bambada Press, 1995), and *Stalking the Demon: Tales of Sex and Insanity* (Jacobyte Books, 2002).

"Kuraria" made his first appearance in print with "The Seamounts of Vaalua Tuva," in *Cthulhu Deep Down Under* (Horror Australis, 2015; reprinted in two volumes by IFGW Australia 2017/2018). A follow-up tale, "*Kōpura* Rising," describing a malign, marine-dwelling race named Kōpura, appeared in *Cthulhu: Land of the Long White Cloud* (IFGW, 2018), a volume collecting all–New Zealand tales of the Cthulhu Mythos. Bryce Stevens was a co-editor of this series of Cthulhu Mythos anthologies. (*Cthulhu Deep Down Under 3* appeared around October 2021.) *"Kōpura* Rising" was selected as a finalist for the 2018 Australian Aurealis Awards for Best Horror Novella and added to Ellen Datlow's 2018 *Best Horror of the Year* recommended reading list. Kuraria also has a recent tale, "The Phobia Clinic," in Deborah Sheldon's anthology *Spawn: Weird Horror Tales about Pregnancy, Birth and Babies* (IFGW, 2021).

David Kuraria's *Bedding the Lamia* is a varied collection, its stories ranging across horror of the weird, macabre, and psychologically horrific types, as well as the grotesquely humorous. Luke Spooner's cover art and design, in shades of bilious green, perfectly conveys the feel and look of the humidity, treacherous swamps, and creeping vines of Kuraria's tropic climes. *Bedding the Lamia* undoubtedly deserves a proud place on your horror bookshelf.

A Journey through Time and Lovecraft

Greg Gbur

JONATHAN THOMAS. *Avenging Angela and Other Uncanny Encounters*. New York: Hippocampus Press, 2021. 254 pp. $20.00 tpb. ISBN 9781614983415 (paperback). ISBN 9781614983514 (ebook).

Though short tales of weird fiction are usually born of a single starting inspiration, some authors are especially good at tracking down unusual ideas—from science, philosophy, or history—and building extremely compelling stories exploring the implications of those concepts. For me, part of the joy of reading such stories is the thrill of discovery: the revelatory moment when the hidden idea underlying the narrative makes itself clear.

This is the impression I had reading Jonathan Thomas's *Avenging Angela and Other Uncanny Encounters,* published in October 2021 by Hippocampus Press. This collection, Thomas's sixth, is a delightful variety of fourteen tales that span genres and provide plenty of surprises, often with strange and thoughtful concepts at their core.

An example of a story built on a clever concept is "One Across," in which a psychiatrist attempts to work with an institutionalized patient with an uncanny knack for finding alternative solutions to crossword puzzles. The story is clearly inspired by the so-called Mandela effect, a psychological phenomenon in which many people share a false memory of an event that never happened, like civil rights leader Nelson Mandela dying in prison or a collection of children's books being titled "Berenstein" instead of the correct "Berenstain." In "One Across," Thomas spins a tale in which the patient may in fact only be a guest in our reality.

Another example of a clever concept story is "The Muybridge Cocktail," named after Edweard Muybridge, the first person to successfully photograph a galloping horse. Muybridge's photographs showed that a horse in gallop will have all its feet off the ground at the same time, solving a debate that had been running among artists and horse enthusiasts for years. Building on the observation that some prehistoric cave paintings seem to have gotten this depiction of horses in motion correct, Thomas tells the story of an archaeologist who discovers the secret of the primitive man's artwork—and tests it on himself, with disastrous results.

Stories set in ancient times are one of the highlights of the collection. The first story of the book, "The Shaman's Smile," is set in a Neolithic village that must contend with the horrors of restless dead as well as an unscrupulous shaman. In "Grave Days in Skara Brae," mystics that are trained to see with supernatural sight are unprepared for the moment when someone stares back at them. "After the Legions" is set in England soon after the departure of the Roman legions. A Roman noble, checking on the status of his estate, finds himself caught in a conflict that arose in the power vacuum of Rome's departure.

Several of the stories in the collection are inspired by Lovecraft's mythos in intriguing ways, and are even inspired by Lovecraft himself. "The Once and Future Waite" begins with a doctor delving into the history of a sanitarium room that wreaks a terrible psychological toll on any occupant. Though not obvious at first, the story is thoroughly Lovecraftian, and I laughed out loud in delight when the connection finally revealed itself to me partway through.

Two stories in the collection feature Lovecraft himself. In "A Box from Blackstone," a modern resident of Lovecraft's old neighborhood learns of a legend that Lovecraft hid a box with mysterious contents nestled within the cracks of an ancient stone wall. The contents of this box turn out to be astounding and unexpected. (Again, this is a story where one can pick out the really clever idea that inspired it, though I will not spoil that here.)

The title story of the collection, "Avenging Angela," features Lovecraft as a character. Howard Phillips Lovecraft teams up with Harry Houdini to solve the mystery of a man who seems to be haunted by the ghost of a former lover. This story is perhaps my favorite of the collection, and the characters of Lovecraft and Houdini are brought to life in the telling. This story gives us a hint of Jonathan Thomas's feelings toward the somewhat problematic author: Lovecraft is depicted as a brilliant man, but with hints of deep personal flaws. The story is obviously based on the real-life short-lived collaboration between Houdini and Lovecraft, and it left me wanting more fictional investigative team-ups between the two.

Avenging Angela and Other Uncanny Encounters is a very strong collection, featuring an impressively diverse range of stories where the reader is never quite sure where the next tale in the volume will take them. It left me wanting more, and wondering where Thomas will take us next.

Absence Makes the Heart Grow Colder

Daniel Pietersen

HELEN DE GUERRY SIMPSON. *The Outcast and the Rite: Stories of Landscape and Fear, 1925–1938.* Edited by Melissa Edmundson. Bath, UK: Handheld Press, 2022. 252 pp. £12.99 (UK); $17.99 (US) tpb. ISBN: 9781912766604.

In the essay "Some Remarks on Ghost Stories," written only a few years after the majority of the stories in this volume were published, M. R. James briefly discusses the concept of "reticence" as it relates to the disquieting tale. James defines reticence, quite literally the act of "remaining silent," by contrasting it with blatancy and, allowing himself no small amount of condescension, those stories which he considers to be "merely nauseating." The doorway left slightly ajar, the figure standing silently at the edge of a forest, "the stony grin of unearthly malice." These are all what James calls "the backbone of a ghost story." This may seem obvious to more modern readers—the concept of "less is more" is so familiar to us that it has become cliché—but there is a less obvious layer to this concept of reticence. To understand it we must move beyond reticence as that which is "not said," elements that are simply left out of the narrative, to that which is "unsaid"; to a place where silence is not simply a passive lack of substance but an active void of implied possibility. Those things that are unsaid, starkly defined by the gap they leave due to their absence, are as much a kind of ghost as any sheeted form or clanking chains.

Helen de Guerry Simpson, in the eerily oblique tales collected here by Melissa Edmundson, is one writer whose understanding of this deeper reticence, this unsettling failure of absence, is often masterful.

Simpson, as Edmundson's introduction outlines, was a remarkable woman. Born at the end of the nineteenth century in Australia she studied at Oxford and, during the First World War, her facility with languages led her to become an interpreter and decoder for the Woman's Royal Naval Service. Although she had initial hopes of becoming a musician, her writing proved popular and she eventually gained admission to the hallowed Detection Club alongside the likes of Agatha Christie and Dorothy L. Sayers, who would be a close friend of Simpson's until the latter's early death from cancer in 1940. Simpson was also a great scholar of witchcraft and the occult—Sayers recalls how her friend would read the Tarot on request—but she maintained a pragmatic view of magical practice, which again shows her understanding of how the things unsaid can be as powerful as those said; "You can't move mountains by faith," she admits in a previously unpublished speech discovered by Edmundson. "You can, however, once you've got into the microcosm, the little world of which man's mind is the governor, lay about you and change things there."

These things unsaid linger in Simpson's stories. The young narrator of "As Much More Land" sneaks into an allegedly haunted room in order to debunk the oblique horrors that are said by his hostess Anne to wait within. His initial bravado starts to wane, however, once he is actually inside the white-painted room: "White, he ponders. 'It's distressing to consider how we are obsessed by it, and how it persists in decoration. Because really it is a negation, a denial'"—and his mind starts to fill the empty space with the horrors he had initially dismissed. The whole story pivots around the failed absence of knowledge haunting the narrator. "So there must be something," he asserts when his interest in the room starts to build. "It's possible that I don't know the whole story; she may have left out some detail, kept something back." Equally, he later assigns the fear he starts to feel in the room to the suggestion that there *should* be something to fear; "If Anne hadn't told me, I should have felt nothing." Whether there is something in the room, possibly even the room itself, to be afraid of is beside the point if the gap created by that something's absence causes fear in itself. "The story may be a lie, but the feeling's authentic."

"Grey Sand and White Sand," a tale of marshlands and madness that comes across as a very early example of what we now call folk horror, similarly uses absence—the silences that exist between people too close to become strangers as much as the wide, featureless expanses of land and sea and sky—to build tension and then horror. Here we find Hilary Monk painting and repainting the bleak vistas that lie beyond his small cottage even as "he knew well enough that they were only tricks of light and shadow; a series of masks." He guards his obsession with the landscape jealously, especially from "the woman who lived with him, to whom he referred for convenience as his wife." Very little happens for the majority of this slight story, but the few events that do occur exist in a field of electric potential. As the couple eat a meager meal, Simpson states that "outwardly they were both calm" and immediately introduces the possibility of what they might be feeling inwardly, what turmoil might writhe under their unruffled exteriors. When this turmoil finally breaks through the shell of Hilary Monk it does so in a way that is deeply unsettling with the vast, unspoken possibilities of the line "then he noticed the fields."

There are many other excellent pieces in this collection—such as "Disturbing Experience of an Old Lady," a quieter cousin to Shirley Jackson's *The Haunting Of Hill House,* or the weirdly off-kilter riddle of "The Pledge," which would fit well next to one of Camilla Grudova's surreally angular tales—but I have to admit that they are not for everyone. Simpson expects her readers to work, to pick away at the story behind the story, rather than simply stroll along until the ghost appears, the murderer is revealed, or even the tentacles erupt from some nameless abyss. Even "A Curious Story," one of Simpson's more straightforward tales of presences that should be absent, has a frustrating sense that there must be something more to it, some hidden layer of meaning that tempts us as the haunted room tempts the nameless narrator of "As Much More Land."

The stories in *The Outcast and the Rite* are not always tales of haunting, but they are all haunting tales. They linger in the mind not despite but entirely because of their suggestiveness and occasional incompleteness. It is hard not to feel Simpson's presence somewhere nearby; a presence that—like the figure in the cover image, Louis Popineau's *Lady in Park*—only beckons us deeper in with its silence.

Another excellent and highly recommended addition to Handheld's library of unfairly ignored but deeply weird tales.

Lamb of God

Michael D. Miller

Lamb. Valdimar Jóhannsson, dir. A24, 2021.

The folk horror revival is alive and well, as evidenced by a slew of such films in recent years, including Iceland's *Lamb* (2021), directed by Valdimar Jóhannsson. This film offers a unique take on the genre through a minimalistic approach and subsequent Scandinavian existentialism. *Lamb* is still rooted in the pagan/natural world in contrast with our modern sensibilities, and also weighs that against modern issues with a strong theme of acceptance; but this film handles it with more subtlety than similar films such as *Titane* or *Pig* (both 2021). Overall the film has a weirdness all its own and worth experiencing.

For the folk horror element, *Lamb* immerses us in a harsh rural setting, a farm, and the relation to livestock. This is one of the significant aspects of the film's minimalism—an isolated farmstead in Iceland, with only three principal characters, and the lambs. The cinematography is lush and beautiful, and the sounds are slight and naturalistic, almost as if this were a documentary of daily life for the two herders, the married couple, María (Noomi Rapace) and Ingvar (Hilmir Snær Guðnason). This is a masterful choice by Jóhannsson as it sets up the audience for the weirdness to come. Thematically the move is perfect as we experience María and Ingvar practice the art of raising sheep and administering birth, yet struggle to have children of their own.

The film's opening sequence is an ominous foreshadowing of the denouement to come. We see through the point-of-view of an unknown force as it moves across the countryside and creeps into the farmstead as sheep run in fear except one lone female. The point-of-view closes on her expression and fades out. Soon enough, this sheep gives birth to a half-human hybrid, although we see very little of this. María and Ingvar take the offspring into their home to care for it. The mother sheep continues to weep for her stolen offspring. At the mid-point of the film, we see the lamb-child in a full shot, one of the most startling reveals in recent cinema. This lamb-child is portrayed perfectly, not letting us know if it knows what it is. The lamb-child seems to take to domestication quite well, but acquiring this child of their own begins to unsettle María and Ingvar and push them to the edge. María shoots the dam to stop her incessant crying. Ingvar's brother Pétur (Björn Hlynur Haraldsson) visits the farm, giving us an outsider's view on the situation, refusing to accept this hybrid-child. Then in the final act the "father" returns, a goat-man of some sort, to collect the child and avenge the mother sheep with a sacrifice of his choosing.

Lamb has much thematic content compressed into this simple story. The film certainly speaks to the older classic mythological themes and animal-human hybrids. Divine births often occurred between human females and the god Zeus in many various animal forms. There is also the legend of the Minotaur itself, unnaturally conceived when Pasiphaë was impregnated by a bull, the ultimate hybrid, kept alive to prey upon those sacrificed by King Minos in his underground maze. There is such divine birth in Norse mythology as well, with the god Loki taken on various forms to beget hybrid creatures and other monstrosities such as the Midgard Serpent. The film also alludes to the ultimate divine birth, that of Jesus Christ and the miracle pregnancy of the virgin Mary. Until the conclusion of the film, the birth of the hybrid-lamb plays off all these examples, with the offspring all accepted in one way or another by their societies.

Other themes the film embraces seem best brought out in the horror genre. Acceptance is tested when we are shown the hybrid form of the monstrosity. Despite the weirdness of this possibility, through domestication and child development of the parents we come to accept this in a strange uneasy way. The film also investigates the nature of parenting and its many responsibilities and challenges. How much do they give the child? How much does the focus on the child take over other responsibilities? How much does the desire to have a child at any cost convey a moral framework? We can see that desire overwhelm María, Ingvar, and even Pétur to the point where murder to keep that child is sanctioned. The old Scandinavian theme of "sin punishes sin" or in other articulations "divine retribution" is preserved. Whatever the sheep-hybrid race is, whatever it means, the visit, the impregnation, the birth, and the revenge all carry out that theme in tragic but deserved ways.

Lamb touches on many other themes, relationships between husband and wife, mother and father, child and parents, siblings, infidelity, isolation, and the other. This particular film manages to carry it out in a minimalistic, natural, and controlled pace that always leaves the audience never knowing what is going to happen. It casts an immersive spell that works because its technique is believable without judgment. This is certainly one of the most naturalistic films of the year and fits the folk horror theme. Folk horror is often mixed with religious horror, especially in an opposed pagan/Christian context; and this film delivers a religious message as well, through its rural pagan atmosphere that might be the most horrific moment of all. The message is easy: "Lamb of God, you take away the sins of the world, grant us peace."

A World Tour of Folk Horror

Jonathan Berman

Woodlands Dark and Days Bewitched: A History of Folk Horror.
Kier-La Janisse, dir. Severin Films, 2021.

Gentle reader: create a list of objects that warm your heart. Read
that list out loud often, for if you live and breathe it will soon carry
you out of the fog and into the light.
This imagined command could easily be the celestial
marching orders for the intriguing documentary *Woodlands*
Dark and Days Bewitched, which is both blessed and cursed by
its earnest exuberance in seemingly sharing every folk horror
film ever made.

What is a "folk horror" film, anyway? Director Kier-La
Janisse terms it "a horror film that takes place almost always in
a rural environment that deals to some degree with folk customs, practices or beliefs." Her documentary lovingly melds
fifty interviewees and 200 films into a scholarly yet accessible
survey. Janisse knows her stuff; she is a film writer, program-
mer, publisher, producer, and founder of the popular
Miskatonic Institute of Horror Studies, an educational venue
with branches in Montreal, New York, Los Angeles, and
online.

The cinematic subgenre of folk horror is centered upon a
"new wave" of horror films that began in the 1970s. They of-
fered a critical response to Hammer's hollow Gothic film output, while anticipating the violence and misogyny of Sam
Peckinpah's Westerns. Thematically, however, folk horror
films eschewed Peckinpah's nihilism, instead offering a full-
throated counter-cultural critique of midcentury "progress."

Woodlands Dark and Days Bewitched starts by introducing
us to the holy triumvirate of folk horror cinema. These are
Witchfinder General (1968, dir. Michael Reeves), which features Vincent Price as a psychotic witch hunter; *The Wicker*
Man (1973, dir. Robin Hardy), a cult film favorite; and *The*

Blood on Satan's Claw (1971, dir. Piers Haggard), which in the *New York Times*'s original review connects us to a possible literary inspiration for the film and the genre:

> . . . it has a good deal of the quality of an H. P. Lovecraft work, in the vulnerability of even its heroic characters, as well as in its pastoral landscape that contains the threat of "eeveel" within every sun-dappled glade. Most particularly, it contains Lovecraft's perfectly straight-faced acceptance of a universe whose natural order may, at any time, be overturned by supernatural disorder.

Watching the documentary feels like taking a full semester course in one three-hour swoop, albeit a course blessed with a bountiful and pleasurable visual harvest. The lush transfers of 35mm films will make you remember why film trumps video, with a gorgeous mise-en-scène that tempts us with yellow-haired and white-skinned willowy maidens; slowly waving green and brown pastoral fields; and stark black and white depictions of secret rural ceremonies.

Woodlands Dark and Days Bewitched explores the genre's roots in a weighty section entitled "Who Is This, Who Is Coming? Signposts of British Folk Horror." M. R. James (1862–1936) figures heavily as a source for the genre. His ghost stories often present a visiting scholar studying in a remote village, only to find an object that unlocks an unholy secret. "Two ingredients most valuable in the concocting of a ghost story are, to me, the atmosphere and the nicely managed crescendo," which ultimately reveal a malevolent presence, according to James. Folk horror films abide by James's counsel while emphasizing themes such as urban encroachment upon the rural (bad!), and patriarchal logic as a foolhardy attempt to bludgeon ancient wisdom. Sharp connections are made to British documentaries and television series (including *Dr. Who*) that highlight narrative and thematic similarities among the works.

Janisse has assembled a quirky crew of knowledgeable scholars who win us over with their passion: they love what they do and that is more than enough. One such collaborator is American Indian critic and curator Jesse Wente, who bristles at the cliché of the Indian burial ground as claptrap, noting that each tribe has its own customs, but he soon warms to the idea: "If non-indigenous people are afraid, great, because it [North America] is all an Indian burial ground." A sequence on zombies takes on hoodoo versus voodoo, Boris Karloff, and the symbolic meanings of moribund sleepwalkers. Janisse enters the fray as on-camera talent, employing a newish documentary trend, the director self-interview, which handily fills in narrative gaps. Filmmaker Guy Maddin offers paper collages that have been dynamically animated by Zena Grey and Brendt Rioux. Jim Williams contributes a haunting score, and the soundtrack draws from many sources, opening with The Undead's trippy version of *Magpie* ("Devil, Devil I Defy Thee . . .").

Where the film falters is in trying to expand its reach globally, as we begin to wear from the sheer weight of what soon becomes a hurried journey. Whereas many of today's bloated documentary series would be better served as a single film, *Woodlands Dark and Days Bewitched* might play better as a series, decisively chopped, if you will, into more digestible bites.

Should you then, dear reader, indulge in *Woodlands Dark and Days Bewitched*? If your virtual walk upon England's mountain green dissolves into teatime with the devil, and you see candlelight flickering across dark woods and children dancing in the shadows, then you must. Watch the film because: what if the old ways are right after all?

A Cavalcade of Death

Donald Sidney-Fryer

CATHERINE PRENDERGAST. *The Gilded Edge: Two Audacious Women and the Cyanide Triangle That Shook America.* New York: Dutton, 2021. 352 pp. $28.00 hc. ISBN 978-0-59-318292-5.

For anyone seriously interested in California's Bohemian scene—the late 1800s and early 1900s—this remarkable monograph is a must-read, the author's "first work of narrative nonfiction." *The Gilded Edge* is an adroit but accurate pun on "The Gilded Age."

Prendergast has done a helluva job of search, research, compiling, shaping, and editing. Apart from a few salient speculations, the book is a substantial and hard-won piece of labor, deserving of respect and admiration. As a professor of English, the author appears as a perfectly capable, competent, and professional writer, occasionally loosening up what seems like a proper scholastic style with the occasional direct colloquialism. This results in a vivid and compelling narration.

Apart from the few major extrapolations, she fills in any gap or lacuna logically and plausibly. She thus brings to life an earlier period of literary and artistic ferment and genuine accomplishment. Since we, the author-critic, tend to judge writers on their writing per se and not the pitiful or pathetic details of their personal existence, this monograph provides a significant revelation about George Sterling, Jack London, James Hopper, and Henry Lafler. Their dealings with women left much to be desired—a gross understatement!

One could say that Prendergast turns a sharp feminist eye, a bright light or focus, on the Bohemia of a hundred years or so a-gone. But that would be to mischaracterize her book. She is merely telling the truth as it revealed itself during her search or research. What search or tool has she not used, and to good effect? We personally found much of her revelation disillusioning, but that's okay. Before reading this book, we had no concept of what a "shit" Sterling could be, or Jack London for that matter, in their dealings with women. What a shock!

Perhaps we should not judge them harshly. The historical period in which they lived dictated some of their behavior, but we cannot blame the period alone for that. Certain entrenched attitudes and customs had their overwhelming part to play. To many men, women "were still only potential conquests or crones, a Madonna-whore complex on a national scale." And people considered this as normal or usual! Women in general tended to be ignored.

They were "buried" in archives under some man's name, but not on their own. "They were buried because their personal histories exposed events and insights far too revealing of the flaws of the men who surrounded them." What an indictment of our overall human history! Let us now examine certain issues as they come up in the course of the tale as told by Prendergast.

The main thing of importance between the sexes, of people making love, inhered in pregnancies, wanted or unwanted. And in the latter case, the strict laws against abortion had to be faced. Women had to travel abroad to secure one, or induce one on their own, which could lead to their demise. Thus it turned out as a stern matter of life and death, as it did in the case of Nora May French. She loved men, and she loved making love with them. A passionate woman, she unavoidably had several abortions. She did not want to be a parent.

Another factor at play in this earlier Bohemia: whenever people grew tired of the thrill of life, they could simply take a tiny amount of cyanide of potassium and end their existence. It appears that many in that early Bohemia of San Francisco and Carmel carried a small vial of cyanide, or they could easily get it from a pharmacy, or illicitly. Presumably no big deal.

Let us deal first with the one major speculation or extrapolation made by Prendergast. I knew Nora's sister Helen French Hunt as a personal friend from summer 1968 to summer 1973 (when she died). I cannot credit that George Sterling had a clandestine romance or affair with Nora. One of the first questions that I asked her when we met was whether either of them had ever made love with George, given his philandering. A prime question! Helen answered forthrightly: "No." At that late date she would not have lied; there was no need. It was ancient history. When George could not seduce some women friends, he then henceforth regarded them as sisters, as he did both Nora and Helen. See line 1 of stanza 2 of "The Ashes in the Sea: N. M. F.": "Such as a sister's was thy brow."

For Prendergast, ancient history or not, the question remains: what was, or is, the source of her speculation about George and Nora? At least one of the later articles from the local press, Carmel or Monterey, mentions Nora as dying for love of George Sterling. Strategically, no letters exist to testify "to their intimacies." Prendergast could find no surviving ones between the two, if in fact any were written. They had no need for them. They lived close enough to communicate in person and had no need to write, never mind to manage a clandestine love affair that thus never happened. Helen has borne witness to that.

1907: Nora commits suicide at last, after having mentioned the possibility many times and trying to do so at least once; it proved a failure. Her body was reduced to ashes at a San Francisco crematorium. Her closest friends held a ceremony on Point Lobos, and George threw the urn into the ocean, the ashes of her *and* her child, but only Carrie Sterling suspected it at the time. The suicide with ceremony was reported in many newspapers across the nation.

Her sister Helen attended, of course, and later asserted that Nora was "over-sexed" and brought her dilemma on herself. An honest evaluation. If anyone would know, it was her sister.

1915: The Panama-Pacific Exposition, celebrated statewide from San Diego to San Francisco. The City created what became the later Marina District by filling in some tidal flats north of the main city area: overall some 600 acres later liberated for housing development. The expo buildings included the Palace of Machinery, 2 miles long, so large that a plane had flown through it! Bernard Maybeck's Palace of Fine Arts is still in place. The Tower of Jewels is more than 400 feet high and decorated with some 100,000 pieces of colored crystal. The City had completely recovered or recuperated after the earthquake and fire of 1906, and California had certainly come of age as demonstrated both in San Francisco and San Diego, even if Jack London died in November 1916, primarily caused by lifelong alcoholism.

1918: Carolyn Rand, Mrs. Carrie Sterling, dies of cyanide in a glass of water, another death by cyanide that many Bohemians carried in little vials. The Cavalcade of Death continues forward. Meanwhile Nora's death continues to haunt George. He writes several poems to her memory. Prendergast seems to cover all the issues, researching and searching in depth.

Sterling dies in November 1926, also a death by cyanide. What had he accomplished? Quite a few volumes of poetry and poetic dramas later collected and republished in three big volumes by Hippocampus Press in 2013.

In 1982, the city of San Francisco installed a George Sterling memorial bench in the park at Lombard St. and renamed it the George Sterling Park. Bench and park remain, a fitting reminder of the earlier Bohemia dominated by the City's own poet laureate.

1927: The Cavalcade of Death continues, but not through a vial of cyanide this time. Herman Scheffauer had returned to his native Germany, and he stabbed to death Katherine von Mayer, his secretary and twenty-three-year-old lover. Then he threw himself to his death out the window. In the end, Scheffauer showed himself as much of a "shit" as Sterling and the Socialist-sainted Jack London, whose books became very popular in Soviet Russia, done into competent Russian translations.

Meanwhile the novelist Mary Austin (1868–1934) outlived all those other early Bohemians and left a solid legacy of more than twenty books, including her autobiography, *Earth Horizon,* and especially *The Land of Little Rain,* which remains an exceptional volume to this day. She is the only woman of that earlier Bohemia whose work and reputation have survived in good or great shape, that is, apart from Nora May French and her poetry.

Prendergast has done magnificent justice in a fair-handed manner to a wide range of published authors in her wide-ranging monograph. Bravissimo!

A surprise and a disappointment: Prendergast doesn't get Sterling as a poet. "His *Testimony* [*of the Suns*] was an ornate and labored try at an epic poem, overlarded with obscure references and unnecessarily rarified vocabulary, and littered with *thee's, thou's,* and *thines.*" Many people still used these last-cited in writing poetry in the late nineteenth and early twentieth centuries. We should mention here in passing that the disappearance of the true second-person singular represents a significant loss in spoken English. It is the only major language that lacks it, whereas French, Spanish, Portuguese, Italian, and Russian still possess it on a colloquial basis in speech and writing, not to mention Chinese and Japanese.

Further, Prendergast opines that "George's lyrics are, to modern readers, a slog." Perhaps to some, but not to literate and literary folk. Any reader who can easily read the Elizabethans would have no trouble reading Sterling, or Clark Ashton Smith for that matter. And as for comparing his "star poem" to Rudyard Kipling's "Recessional," this was a major mistake on Prendergast's part, like comparing apples to oranges. George was making a salient literary statement in *Testimony*—cosmic-astronomic in application and intent, a statement that had nothing to do with contemporary politics or monarchs.

Sterling employed the same stanza used by Tennyson for *In Memoriam* (as well as by Bierce for his noble "Invocation"). The style and stanza still seemed perfectly relevant at least up to World War I and beyond, into the early 1920s. The Roaring Twenties definitely introduced a new sensibility and taste.

The death of George Sterling by cyanide in November 1926, whether suicidal or accidental—Clark Ashton Smith all his life considered it an accident, that George took it by mistake in the confusion caused by his illness—did indeed mark the end of an epoch, in fact the end of a century, when the nineteenth century itself at last came to an end, culturally and artistically.

Suspension of Belief: A Look Back at James Herbert's *Creed*

Philip Challinor

More than half of the twenty-three novels produced by the English writer James Herbert (1943–2013) over a career of nearly four decades are horror thrillers. Their heroes are usually professional investigators—private or police detectives, security operatives, journalists—and their stories are essentially mystery or suspense plots, with monsters and mutants in place of (or in cahoots with) criminals, foreign agents, fascists, and other all-too-human undesirables. Other of Herbert's books feature such devices of the traditional ghost story as revenants and haunted buildings, but resemble thrillers in favoring plot and set-pieces over atmospheric suggestion; and the protagonist in three of these novels is another professional investigator, albeit one who specializes in the occult. Nevertheless, Herbert did occasionally kick up his heels. His fourth novel, *Fluke* (1977), marketed as a horror story at the publisher's insistence, is a first-person tragicomic picaresque about a man reincarnated as a dog; his twentieth, *Once . . .* (2001), is a disastrous sidestep into fantasy complete with waggish gnomes and crude in-jokes; and his fifteenth, *Creed* (1990), is something else again.

Considered purely in terms of its plot, *Creed* is perfectly conventional. Joe Creed, a paparazzo whose idea of paradise is capturing "something for worldwide syndication" (11), spies on the funeral of a notorious film star and takes some photographs that are, to put it mildly, compromising. As a result, he is variously menaced by mysterious and secretive powers, while receiving ambiguously helpful advice from a pretty girl and being erotically distracted by a *femme fatale*. The villains kidnap the photographer's son, inflict traumatic damage on his cat, and prove at last to be involved in a conspiracy reaching to the very highest echelons of society. Creed traces them to their lair and, with a little help from the good girl and his fellow paparazzi, rescues his son and defeats the evil, at least for now. Such an outline could apply to a mainstream thriller as much as to a supernatural one, and the fact that the villains in this case turn out to be literal fiends is entirely in keeping with the Herbert *oeuvre;* but in *Creed* Herbert adopts several devices that undercut the conventional formula and actively subvert the reader's suspension of disbelief.

Although the book's title and the hero's name connote belief and principle, Joseph Creed is an entirely self-centered, amoral protagonist. His personal ethic is summed up in a trinity of commandments to unfaith: "1) Do unto others before they do unto you; 2) Never trust anyone in authority, ex-wives, lovers, helpful strangers, priests (of any variety); 3) Bend with the wind, and snap back hard in the lulls" (229). Both Creed and his son Samuel have biblical first names associated with faith and virtue; but Creed's person reflects neither the interpreter of dreams in Genesis (our Joseph certainly would never have resisted Mrs. Potiphar's advances) nor the righteous husband in the Gospels. Divorced from his wife and inconsiderate of his child in true action-heroic fashion, Creed is also sadly lacking in that belated devotion to family values which has warmed the emotional climax of many an ordinary thriller. His ex-wife openly resents and despises him, and his son is entirely bereft of the plucky good cheer, premature moral wisdom, and penetrating emotional intelligence that so often characterize troubled genre moppets. Samuel Creed is an overweight sad sack neglected by his father and smothered by his mother: a stark contrast to his prophet namesake, whose mother gave him up to the priesthood and who received regular personal communications from the Father Himself. Having taken out his emotional problems on his junior schoolmates, Sammy is suspended for unauthorized bullying and amateur extortion, which goads his mother into foisting him on the beleaguered hero at a most inconvenient juncture. Abducted as an inducement to Creed's cooperation, he is eventually rescued by his father, not without a reminder about his diet and perhaps not entirely from fear of ex-wifely retribution.

The villains are just about as glamorous as the hero. Formerly an art director at an advertising agency, Herbert designed his own book packaging, and his tagline for *Creed* was "Demons today are a shoddy lot" (6). Although their manifestations convincingly defy natural law, the demons are prone to ludicrous pseudonyms and cheap tricks with anagrams and spiked tobacco; clearly, whatever they may once have possessed in the way of Byronic pride or Miltonic grandeur has fallen to less epic levels. An apparent vampire resembling the ratlike monster in F. W. Murnau's 1922 film *Nosferatu* (Creed has a redeeming fondness for old films) turns out to be a decrepit creature named Bliss who had "begun to believe his own publicity" (314). The leading demon, Belial alias Nicholas Mallik, is a jaded showman and sometime child-murderer; his domain is a rest-home-*cum*-dungeon-*cum*-laboratory haunted by senile hangmen and zombified Hollywood termagants; and the bulk of his followers are summed up by Creed, with characteristic reverence, as "moth-eaten freaks with snake tails and peacock feathers" (312).

Nor is the female lead altogether what one might expect. In a normal thriller narrative, the good girl's function is to help the hero in his quest and assist his emotional reintegration and moral redemption. She usually survives to establish a stable romantic relationship with him, although once in a while an author may offer her up as a sacrifice to motivation when the climax approaches. By contrast, the *femme fatale* is there to distract the hero with lies and half-truths and to addle him with sex appeal; and she often dies at his hands, or occasionally at the villain's after a last-minute change of allegiance. In *Creed* the attractive young blonde woman who tries to aid and protect the hero turns out to be the same entity as the voluptuous raven-haired succubus who perversely seduces him, and she also confesses to a particularly disgusting vice: "I'm afraid the human condition has always been one of my failings" (316). According to Ramsey Campbell (264), Herbert himself described *Creed* as his *Abbott and Costello Meet Frankenstein,* and the 1945 original does indeed feature blonde Jane Randolph in the virtuous female role and dark-haired Lenore Aubert in the villainous one.

The tool of Creed's trade is an instrument that has been said never to lie, but which literally and metaphorically frames its subjects and unavoidably misleads by omission. Nor is Creed's vocation the widely respected and sometimes informative trade of photo-journalist, but merely the catching of famous persons at embarrassing moments for sensational display in a British tabloid. Even in 1990, British tabloids were not exactly by-words for honesty, seriousness, or truth: as the narrative says, "To protect the not-so-innocent, we'll call the tabloid *The Daily Dispatch* (although *The Daily Rumour, Gup,* or *Gospel* might be as appropriate)" (25). That last is especially piquant in light of the self-justifying assertion by the reporter protagonist of Herbert's earlier novel *Shrine* (1983) that "Jesus Christ hired twelve pretty good PR guys to spread the word, four of whom wrote a world-wide bestseller" (134).

Herbert was a Roman Catholic; and although *Shrine* takes a less indulgent view of the Church than William Peter Blatty in *The Exorcist,* Herbert's attachment to Christian moralism is apparent throughout his work. The hero of *Domain* (1984) blames nuclear holocaust not on a ruthless and bungling geopolitical élite but on "the stark face of ultimate evil . . . The destructive force that was centuries-old and inherent in every man, woman and child! God forgive us all" (36). In equally dubious vein, homosexual acts, and even homosexual desires that are never acted upon, in many Herbert novels virtually guarantee a gruesome set-piece demise; but *Creed* is less inclined toward this regrettable portent. One victim of Creed's camera is a macho actor with a weakness for rent-boys, but he appears in only one scene and the story has better things to do than kill him off. The bitchily effete diarist at *The Daily Dispatch* does meet a nasty end, but we are informed via a suitably gossipy aside that, despite his stereotypical affectations and some long-ago dalliances in the upper-crust British military, he is in fact asexual; and even Creed, who detests him, concedes that "nobody deserves what they did to you" (265).

Despite such rare displays of a softer side, Creed is not perceptibly altered, let alone improved, by his brush with supernatural peril. As a knowledgeable character observes, "You won't change, Joe. Perhaps it was your low-life nature that ultimately got you through all this" (317). The novel's last scene finds him rationalizing away his more unprofitable feelings, anticipating the payouts for his story, and planning to market some of the less explicit shots from the cemetery reel that started all the trouble.

Like much popular fiction, *Creed* incorporates into its narrative various well-known brand names and personal names from the real world. Besides such notables as Jack Nicholson, Woody Allen, and the Duchess of York, there are brief appearances or mentions of numerous other persons of transient or lasting fame, as well as two real paparazzi whose names are featured in Herbert's acknowledgments at the beginning of the book. In the context of *Creed,* even an in-joke about Herbert's own first novel—"Didn't he read somewhere that rats were taking over the city? Good idea for a book there. Somebody ought to do it" (48)—manages to be more amusing than irritating. For once the real-world references serve a thematic purpose beyond facile winking at the reader: in a story concerned with belief and unbelief, they foreground the average bestseller's tick-box verisimilitude even as the conventions of realism are blatantly undermined by the novel's most radical device.

The most unusual aspect of *Creed* is its highly obtrusive narrative voice, which asserts itself from the beginning and continues throughout to address the reader directly, referring to Creed as "our hero" or "our boy" and providing largely unflattering commentary on his actions and character. Like Herbert's first-person (and favorite) novels *Fluke* and *The Magic Cottage* (1986), *Creed* is written in a relaxed, conversational style, with more overt humor and less of the sometimes stilted diction that mars the third-person majority. Herbert's use of the obtrusive narrator allows him to have his storyteller's cake and eat it too: he can avail himself of third-person omniscience, relating events about which the main character may neither know nor care, without giving up the first-person informality that he evidently found congenial. Perhaps unfortunately, Herbert made no further attempts to exploit this advantage. After *Creed,* he made more conventional use of the first person in *'48* (1996), *Others* (1999), and *Nobody True* (2003); and although the latter two have fairly unconventional narrators—one deformed, the other dead—none of his later novels undercuts its own reality as *Creed* does.

Even in stretches where the thriller plot predominates, the narrator's presence makes itself felt in chatty touches like starting a chapter with "You know" (56) or "Time to interrupt" (75) or "If you've ever paid a visit to a lunatic asylum" (245). Elsewhere, the narrator drops in to editorialize on such matters as the mutual parasitism of paparazzi and politicians, the pains and duties of fatherhood, and the supreme scariness of Murnau's vampire, and he pops up (frequently in snide little parentheses) to elaborate a point or simply to crack wise. When the hero hopes that a disappointing day will be followed by a livelier night, a bracketed codicil gloats, "Oh Creed, if you only knew" (27). After one chapter ends in a cliffhanger, with Bliss breaking the vampire rules by advancing on Creed through running water, the next chapter commences with the smug pronouncement "You've just suffered a dramatic pause" (151) and then helpfully explains the purpose of same. Introducing the novel's final scene, the narrator handily sums up the moral: "Creed has shown that it's not only the bold, the brave and the noble who can achieve a result: sometimes a little rottenness can too" (306).

Though generally about as shy with expletives as one would expect from a stalwart of the press, Creed habitually swears by Judas rather than Jesus, to the extent of using the epithet "Judas Christ" (32, 113). As a euphemism this leaves something to be desired: it suggests not so much a wish to avoid taking the Savior's name in vain as a difference of opinion about who the Savior might have been. The idea of the betrayer as Christ has been convincingly if fictitiously argued by the heretical theologian Nils Runeberg in Jorge Luis Borges's "Three Versions of Judas"; and while one may doubt Creed's acquaintance with that story, it certainly makes the point about the kind of result a little rottenness can achieve. Its epigraph from T. E. Lawrence, "There seemed a certainty in degradation" (Borges 132), could serve as Nicholas Mallik's personal motto.

To a religious sensibility built on faith and reverence, there can be few greater horrors than immortality ludicrously degraded by a mortal lack of belief. Parasitically dependent on humanity's diminishing resources of faith, the forces of supernatural darkness fear oblivion through human skepticism, and one object of their fiendish conspiracy is to force Creed, the ultimate materialist, into becoming a believer. Demons are not the only ones afflicted by the credulity crisis: "the powers of Light are as diminished as the powers of Darkness if they're not accepted" (314). Laughter is arguably as effective an instrument of degradation as fear; and while Herbert's other books are by no means devoid of intentional humor, none of them uses it so pervasively as *Creed,* which is at least as much a comic novel as it is a horror thriller. Thanks to the hero's near-total lack of concern for others, there is little incentive for the reader to suffer vicariously on his behalf; and the supporting cast is presented with a similar dearth of sentiment. When Samuel is kidnapped, Creed's foremost concern is to protect himself from his ex-wife, and his frantic efforts to keep the truth from her are played for laughs. As in *Fluke,* there is a prominent vein of slapstick: the hero concusses himself by tripping over the cat and is carnivorously menaced by a predatory toilet bowl. There is also verbal humor, as when Creed unthinkingly refers to Mallik as "old Nick" (163) or plays interminably daft variations on the surname of one Daniel Lidtrap. Further material emerges from the daily doings of Creed's profession, with lurking crowds of photographers outfoxed in style by canny celebrities, while Creed pays back a personal enemy by gluing his car door shut. In a final glorious anticlimax, the demons are defeated by the less-than-holy light of flashes from the press mob's clicking cameras. Even the cat is called Grin: an expression finely balanced between the fun and friendly and the macabre and mad.

Ramsey Campbell has suggested that the narrator's voice in *Creed* is that of the author speaking directly to the reader, in a manner "almost Victorian" (264). I'm not sure how nearly Victorian a narrator might be who could follow an exuberant sex scene with mention of a "second coming" (221), with or without asking pardon for the pun. Certainly Herbert's narrator is free of such postmodern affectations as entering into dialogue with the characters, taking an active part in the story, or stating explicitly that he is making the whole thing up. Nor, despite his insistent presence, does the narrator ever identify or talk about himself. Rather, he adopts a position of humorous detachment, relating and commenting on events without overtly influencing them or admitting to an agenda of his own; much like the more self-satisfied class of journalist. A cynic might even suspect that *Creed*'s narrator—omniscient yet detached, blithely judgmental, dependent on faith yet continually challenging it, and complaining that "Women aren't easy to understand" (8)—may in truth be the Author and Editor of all being, making His presence felt just in case.

Works Cited

Borges, Jorge Luis. *Fictions*. Tr. Andrew Hurley. London: Penguin, 2000.

Campbell, Ramsey. *Ramsey Campbell, Probably*. Ed. S. T. Joshi. Harrogate, UK: PS Publishing, 2002.

Herbert, James. *Creed*. London: Hodder & Stoughton, 1990.

————. *Domain*. Sevenoaks: New English Library, 1984.

————. *Shrine*. London: Hodder & Stoughton, 1983.

The Problem of Genre Expectation

Géza A. G. Reilly

ELLEN DATLOW, ed. *Body Shocks: Extreme Tales of Body Horror*. San Francisco: Tachyon Publications, 2021. 384 pp. $17.95 tpb. ISBN: 9781636963606.

Body Shocks attempts to be an anthology of stories focusing on the theme of body horror. Although there are a few works of solid body horror present, and there are even more stories that are of merit, the anthology falls short of the mark overall. It is important to stress the point that *Body Shocks* does fail, but it does not do so due to a lack of quality in the stories present. Rather, it fails because it does not sufficiently succeed at the project that has been set for it.

This is a subjective determination, I will admit. Body horror, like all genres, requires a buy-in from the reader along with a quality found in the text itself. For me, however, body horror first and foremost requires a specific location for the "horror" part of the label—the human body. That is, a body horror story is one in which the horror in question comes from *the body itself*. Even if the horror is caused by an outside source, the mutability of the body is the site of the horror rather than the outside cause. In this way, body horror functions by rejecting the Enlightenment humanist perspective of the body as an inviolate subject segregated from the world and other beings around it. The body horror answer to such preconceptions is a monstrously post-humanist one—the body *is not* solid, the subject *is not* inviolate, and the terror, ultimately, is that *we have always already been this way*. Thus, body horror is often allegorical in nature—think of David Cronenberg's *The Fly* and the ways in which it is, underneath the dark science fiction tragedy of its plot, all about the horror of the disintegration of the body due to age, disease, or both. Body horror, therefore, plays with the fears that come from confronting the often porous, always unstable, and universally temporary nature of our bodies.

Editor Ellen Datlow does not present such an understanding of body horror in her introduction to *Body Shocks,* though she does correctly state that body horror "deals with the intimacy of the body's integrity being breached." She cites Phillip Brophy's coining of the term in his article "Horrality: The Textuality of the Contemporary Horror Film" (*Art & Text,* 1983), which is somewhat true in that Brophy used the term "body-horror" to refer to a quality found *within* modern cinematic horror rather than as a genre *of* horror. In his article, Brophy is primarily concerned with defining his theory of "Horrality," which he defines as "a mode of textuality that is dictated by trends within both the Horror genre and cinematic realism." Still, Brophy's passing reference does suggest a nuance that is not present in much of *Body Shocks.* In reference to John Carpenter's *The Thing,* for example, Brophy identifies the titular alien's "total disregard for and ignorance of the human body" and the fact that it "does not honour any of our beliefs or perceptions of what the human body is," which is suggestive of the post-human unsettling of the human as a subject operative within the body horror genre.

Datlow continues in her introduction by giving explicit definitions of body horror by Gabino Iglesias and the Collins Dictionary, but these definitions are superficial and lack any substantive discussion of body horror as a genre (by Iglesias's own admission, his definition is "a hell of a loose description" [*LitReactor,* 2017]). Datlow comes closer to the mark when she quotes Jack Halberstam as arguing that "body horror represents 'the body as a locus of fear.'" However, I was unable to locate that quotation outside of Halberstam's *Skin Shows* (Duke University Press, 1995). There, Halberstam is referring to Mary Shelley's treatment of the body within *Frankenstein* and the Gothic genre; body horror itself is not mentioned in that passage. Better definitions exist even in Halberstam's own work. A much stronger definition, for example, is in Kelly Hurley's "Reading Like an Alien: Posthuman Identity in Ridley Scott's *Alien* and David Cronenberg's *Rabid*" (published in *Posthuman Bodies,* edited by Jack Halberstam [Indiana University Press, 1995]): "The narrative told by body horror again and again is of a human subject dismantled and demolished: a human body whose integrity is violated, a human identity whose boundaries are breached from all sides."

In *Body Shocks,* however, the majority of horrors come solely from *outside* of the human body and focus on what can be done *to* the body rather than the horror and spectacle of "the human body defamiliarized, rendered other" (Hurley). Terry Dowling's "Toother," for example, focuses on a criminal who does rather nasty things to people's teeth. Is this body horror? It strikes me that it is not even by Datlow's own definition, since I see nothing in it that inspires that essential lack of confidence in the body's integrity as a unified whole or inviolate subject. Another example that is perhaps more difficult is "Spores" by Seanan McGuire, which is ultimately an end-of-the-world scenario brought about by a voracious mold that consumes anything and anyone who comes into contact with it. The story therefore does involve horrific things happening *to* human bodies, but I would argue that it does not quite meet the mark of inspiring a fear of our nature as beings embedded in a world of microorganisms constantly (and universally) interpenetrating with what we think of as our solid, individual bodies so much as it inspires a fear of clueless scientists ending the world by mistake.

It is important to keep in mind that neither Dowling's nor McGuire's stories are bad works. The fact is that *Body Shocks* has several stories that are not body horror but are nevertheless strong. Priya Sharma's "Fabulous Beasts," Caitlín R. Kiernan's "Elegy for a Suicide," Lucy Taylor's "Subsumption," and Gemma Files's "Skin City" are just a handful of the stories here that I found quite worth the time spent reading, but I would balk at necessarily categorizing them as body horror. As I've come to expect from her work as an editor, Datlow has a fine eye for quality, and if potential readers are willing to set aside the philosophic and generic expectations in a way that I could not, then they will find a lot of fine fare here.

Even if they cannot, however, there are *some* full-on body horror stories present in *Body Shocks,* and overall they are exceptional (and exceptionally disturbing). Michael Blumlein's "Tissue Ablation and Variant Regeneration: A Case Report," for example, is an abjectly terrifying narrative built on the disassembly of the body and focuses on the confusion of the individual body and the body politic (along with some on-the-nose political satire). Genevieve Valentine's "La Beauté sans Vertu" is a profoundly disturbing investigation of commodification of the body and the dissecting nature of social expectation. And Kij Johnson's "Spar" is perhaps the best interrogation of the body as a solid, inviolate whole that I've read in years (that it is bound up in deeply feminist concerns makes it all the more effective). These stories, however, are in the minority within *Body Shocks,* and I found the disparity between what was promised and what was delivered quite disappointing.

If *Body Shocks* had been presented as a more generalized anthology, I would give it a ringing endorsement without hesitation. It is a fine collection of stories with far fewer misses than hits. As it stands, however, I can only warn potential readers that they might not be receiving what they were looking for, and as a result they might be disappointed by good works in the same way that I was. Body horror is a fascinating genre of horror fiction, and it isn't one that I've seen investigated in print all that often (indeed, I think an argument could be made that it is better suited to film). We are liminal beings, and most of our presumptions about our own individuality, solidity, and general *wholeness* are nothing but comforting illusions. Perhaps we'll receive a modern anthology focusing on those uncomfortable truths eventually, but as it stands, *Body Shocks* simply is not it.

Nobody Puts Baby in the Corner

June Pulliam

Texas Chainsaw Massacre. David Blue Garcia, dir. Bad Hombre/Exurbia Films/Legendary Entertainment, 2022.

The newest installment in the Texas Chainsaw Massacre franchise is very much in the tradition of the newest installments in other well-known slasher franchises such as Halloween and Candyman in its re-imagining of its slashers and original final girls and other survivors. Like Michael Myers and Candyman, Leatherface lives, and presumably is powered by some supernatural force because he must be in his seventies by now but can still swing a chainsaw and smash walls with a sledgehammer, as well as survive gunshot wounds and chainsaw gashes. But David Blue Garcia's *Texas Chainsaw Massacre* is not just another installment in a slasher franchise where the same old monster abides by the same old rules to terrorize another group of young people. Instead, like David Gordon Green's *Halloween* (2018), Garcia's film considers what happened to its original final girl. Like Laurie Strode, Sally Hardesty's life has been shaped by the trauma of watching her friends brutally killed while she lived. While Laurie barricades herself within her fortified compound and amasses an impressive collection of guns, Sally is a Texas Ranger who has spent her entire career searching for Leatherface. Also, Garcia's Leatherface has more understandable reasons for killing than were attributed to him in previous films, making him similar to Nia Da Costa's Candyman in her 2021 film.

In Tobe Hooper's *Texas Chainsaw Massacre,* the east Texas county where Leatherface and the rest of the Sawyer clan reside is dying because the slaughterhouses that once provided residents with a middle-class living now require fewer workers because they kill cattle mechanically. Now, nearly fifty years later, the nearest town in Muerto County, Harlow, has become a ghost town with just two residents—Mrs. MC and

Leatherface. Mrs. MC runs an orphanage where she has taken in children of all ages who were parentless or just needed someone to show them some mercy. Leatherface, who she calls Baby, is the last occupant of this institution, and the frail, elderly woman can control him because she mothers him.

In previous installments in the Texas Chainsaw Massacre franchise, Leatherface kills those who return to Muerto County because they have some distant familial connection there. In Tobe Hooper's original, Sally and her friends have returned to check on her grandfather's grave after hearing about how some of the dead have been disinterred and violated, while in John Lussenhop's *Texas Chainsaw Massacre 3D,* a young woman returns to claim an inheritance. In other installments in the franchise, unlucky hitchhikers end up on the wrong end of Leatherface's chainsaw. But in Garcia's newest installment, most of the characters who come to Harlow are unsympathetic.

Dante, his fiancée Ruth, and their business partner Melody have purchased the town of Harlow and its quaint, disheveled buildings, and will be auctioning them off that day to investors who want to make the town into an upscale tourist destination with pricy cafés, hotels, and even a comic book shop. Melody's younger sister Lila accompanies them and is the only sympathetic one in the group. Before coming to Harlow with her older sister, Lila survived a school shooting at Stoneman High (an obvious reference to the school shooting in Parkland, Florida, at Marjorie Stoneman Douglas High School) and has the bullet scars to prove it. Before the busload of possible investors arrives, however, Melody, Dante, and Ruth enter one of the buildings to remove a tattered Confederate flag hanging from a second-floor window when they discover that all the residents have not left. Mrs. MC is still there and refuses to leave because she claims that she still has the title to the building. (Spoiler alert: she does.) Melody, Dante, and Ruth call the sheriff to have her evicted and tell her condescendingly that "there are places" where people like her can go to be "properly" cared for. Mrs. MC begins to have a heart attack and dies on the way to the hospital, leaving Baby with no one to care for him. Baby kills the three would-be gentrifiers, along with the bus full of investors who have since arrived.

The bus massacre is one of the film's comic moments. When Leatherface boards the bus with his chainsaw, their first instinct is to pull out their phones to livestream the event.

Garcia's *Texas Chainsaw Massacre* is similar to Green's *Halloween* in another way: both create new final girls who take up the mantle of each franchise's original final girl. Melody's sister Lila is uniquely equipped to survive by our modern times. The survivor of a school shooting who believes that she "was supposed to die that day" knows the value of running and hiding. When Ranger Sally Hardesty arrives on the scene, having heard a call for help from one of Leatherface's earlier victims, she advises Lila, "Don't run," because if you do, "he'll never stop haunting you." Unfortunately, Sally's ranger training has not prepared her for someone like Leatherface, and she dies when her gun jams on her, proving the truism of every slasher film: guns are useless. When Lila acquires Sally's shotgun after her death, she shoots Leatherface twice at close range and still doesn't kill him before she has run out of ammo, but it does slow him down for a heartbeat. Melody, who was previously left for dead, comes to her little sister's rescue at the last moment, using Leatherface's chainsaw to deliver what she thinks is the fatal blow to the monster. But as the sisters leave town in their self-driving electric car, Leatherface returns and beheads Melody, who is already making jokes about what they just survived, while Lila helplessly screams through the sunroof as the car drives her out of Harlow.

Garcia's *Texas Chainsaw Massacre* has received a lot of scorn from critics and fans for failing to add anything new to the franchise and its thin characters, but some of this criticism is unfair. I enjoyed seeing how this newest addition to the story has evolved in a way similar to other well-established slasher franchises. True, this *Texas Chainsaw Massacre* isn't as cerebral as the new *Candyman,* but it was fun to see Leatherface live again in an updated situation.

All the Right Reasons

Leigh Blackmore

TERRY DOWLING. *The Complete Rynosseros: The Adventures of Tom Rynosseros*. Art by Nick Stathopoulus. Hornsea, UK: PS Publishing, 2020. Volume 1: 592 pp. £14.99 tpb. ISBN: 9781786366870; Volume 2: 637 pp. £14.99 tpb. ISBN: 9781786366887; Volume 3: 158 pp. £12.99 tpb. ISBN: 9781786366894.

> ". . . there was too much information. Truths were lost. Basic knowledge. How the Information revolution became the Reality Crisis, a saturation of the data-sphere coupled with an intended flattening of affect. Fiction and falsehood more eloquent, more persuasive than available truth."—Terry Dowling, "Coyote Struck by Lightning"

A word about timing. This review is two things. One, it is extremely late in coming. I regret this, but it does not prevent me from wanting, nevertheless, to bring more attention to this incredible set of volumes than it has so far had. Two, it concerns a set of books that is essentially science fiction rather than horror.

Why, then, review it in *Dead Reckonings*? Well, as Sissy Spacek once said about her acting, "It's really about the work—if you are doing it for the right reasons—really to illuminate the human condition." That's what all Dowling's work does. And furthermore, a goodly proportion of this Australian writer's output across the years is horror or dark fantasy, so there is a well-grounded context to *The Adventures of Tom Rynosseros* (or *The Rynosseros Cycle* or *Rynosseros Saga,* depending on which alternative name you prefer to call it by) within Dowling's wider oeuvre that justifies its examination here.

That Terence William Dowling is one of our greatest writers of the *fantastique* is apodeictic. As long ago as the novel *An Intimate Knowledge of the Night* (1995) and the same year's story chapbook *The Man Who Lost Red,* Dowling was exploring dark fantasy and horror as well as science fiction. With his collections *Blackwater Days* (2000), the International Horror Guild Award–winning *Basic Black: Tales of Appropriate Fear* (2006), *Amberjack: Tales of Fear and Wonder* (2010), *The Night Shop: Tales for the Lonely Hours* (2017), and his acclaimed novel *Clowns at Midnight* (2010), which drew comparison to works by such writers as John Fowles, Dowling has continually expanded his palette of formidably intelligent and rewardingly subtextual macabre fiction right alongside his parallel career writing some of the most challenging science fiction of our age.

Now, though critical regard for Dowling's work is extensive—just to cite one ferinstance, *Locus* said: "Who's the writer who can produce horror as powerful and witty as the best of Peter Straub, science fiction as wondrously Byzantine and baroque as anything by Gene Wolfe, near-mainstream subtly tinged with the fantastic like some tales by Powers or Lansdale? Why Terry Dowling, of course" (November 1999)—his name may be an unfamiliar one to some reading this. Partly this will stem from the fact that a number of his books were published only in Australia, and those published in the US or UK have, by and large, appeared as limited or specialist editions. But there is really little excuse for not knowing his horror work. His superb short horror stories have regularly graced the pages of the *Exotic Gothic* series, and a wide variety of anthologies edited by such anthologists of the field as Ellen Datlow. If you need a quick sampler, you could do worse than obtain *Cemetery Dance Select: Terry Dowling* (e-book, 2015), which contains four of his noteworthy tales: "The Daemon Street Ghost-Trap," "The Saltimbanques," "Stitch," and "One Thing about the Night." Or track down a copy of the September/October 2019 issue of *Firsts* magazine, whose lead article is "Terry Dowling: Poet of Shadows," a major piece on Dowling's dark fantasy by American scholar and book collector Boyd White. In White's view, it is "a singularly distinct body of work that is one of the most remarkable achievements in contemporary fantastic fiction."

All that established, *The Complete Rynosseros* represents the culmination in print of a magnificent series of stories set in a vividly imagined far-future Australia. For those new to the saga, the *Australian SF Reader* in October 2007 called it: "The best and most ambitious Australian science fiction series ever written, and one of the best, ever, period." All forty-five Tom Rynosseros stories appear in Volumes 1 and 2 (from the four original Tom collections *Rynosseros, Blue Tyson, Twilight Beach,* and *Rynemonn,* including the near-legendary never-before-collected tale "Marmordesse"; "The Library"; and the long-uncollected "Down Flowers"; plus a brand-new commemorative story, "Calling Down the Sun," written exclusively for this milestone set). Volume 3, *Songs from the Inland Sea,* has been produced exclusively for the PS edition and will delight all long-term enthusiasts of the series, giving as it does a complete illustrated history of Dowling's inspirations for, and experiences with, the writing of the stories, with relevant appendices and ancillary material.

Tom Tyson, an Everyman figure who has echoes of the Fool of the Tarot, Tom O'Bedlam, the Green Man, and other mythic figures have emerged amnesiac from an Ab'O punishment place known as the Madhouse. Tyson becomes one of the "Coloured Captains"—seven Nationals permitted by the Ab'O to cross the landscape—and wins his ship *Rynosseros* in a lottery, thereafter becoming known as Blue Tyson. To quote critic and editor Van Ikin,

> In this future Australia, the coastal cities, home of white Australians, are urbanely cosmopolitan centres of culture, while in the interior, around an inland sea, the Ab'O states represent the emancipation of the Aboriginal race whose heritage is both its past and its future destiny. Ab'O Princes use satellites to spy on tribal conflicts, and graceful wind-propelled sandships roll across the deserts, giving [the series] its symbol of freedom and inquiry.

Dowling has attributed part of the inspiration for the Tom Tyson character to Blue Tyson, a character from one of his high school story fragments, and to the song lyric "Loving Mad Tom" (also known as "Tom O'Bedlam"), which was drawn to his attention by science fiction fan and co-founder of Norstrilia Press, Carey Handfield, in 1982.

In Volume 1, an omnibus collecting the stories from the original first two volumes *Rynosseros* and *Blue Tyson,* we meet Tom Tyson, known widely as Tom "Rynosseros," the Blue Captain, after the sand-ship he wins in the great ship lotteries. He is one of only seven Nationals to have won Hero Colours and fine sand-ships from the rival indigenous tribes that rule Australia with their mastery of high-tech a thousand years from now. We join Tyson and his crew aboard the magnificent kite-drawn charvolant *Rynosseros* as he strives to discover his true identity in a world of strange and dangerous desert states, orbiting battle stations, mind-war, and bizarre terraforming and genetic experiments. Dowling takes us with Tom to the islands of the Inland Sea, to the great sand-ship fighting ground of the Air, to deserted carnivals, haunted artists' colonies, fire-chess contests, and the abandoned arcologies of the continent's interior. Meanwhile he desperately searches for clues to the meaning of the three signs he carries with him from his time in the "Madhouse" among the chattering machines—the signs of a Ship, a Star, and a Woman's Face.

In Volume 2, the second omnibus, which collects all the tales from the original third and fourth Tyson volumes, *Twilight Beach* and *Rynemonn,* events are fast nearing crisis point for the seven Coloured Captains. While Tom continues his quest to learn the meaning of his three Madhouse signs, constantly walking the treacherous line between the interests of the indigenous ruling tribes and those of the white "Nationals" of this far-future Great Southern Land. Roaming the dreamridden streets of Twilight Beach, traveling the strange windriver named the Soul, wandering the Inland Sea's fantastic shores and visiting desert wastes locales such as Totem Rule and Pentecost, Tom Rynosseros by his very presence cannot help but provoke the tribal princes and their powerful allies. By aiding outcasts, travelers, fellow captains, even rogue AI belltrees in his search for his forgotten past, a deadly plan is put in place that will deal with the captains once and for all. In this momentous quest, the question is—will the enigmatic hero Tom Tyson find answers before it's too late? "Calling Down the Sun," a brand-new Tom adventure written exclusively for the PS edition, reveals all-new information that adds special resonance to the entire saga of Rynosseros.

One can only quote the publisher's blurb for Volume 3: *Songs from the Inland Sea*, which is unique to the PS edition and provides an insightful guide to Dowling's history and process as writer over the more than thirty-five years in which he worked on the *Rynosseros* saga, beginning with the tale "Shatterwrack at Breaklight" (published in 1992). "For the completist, the die-hard fan or curious newcomer, *Songs from the Inland Sea* provides an intriguing, heartfelt look at how one writer went about pursuing the dream, and not only added a truly unforgettable character to the canon of modern fantastic literature, but, as often happens in any creative life, came to discover himself in the process." This volume is an utter delight, and provides many crucial insights for readers who have wondered about unanswered aspects of Tom Tyson's life and world. Seeing the series through the lens of Dowling's own reflection on its history—his early life and imaginings even from schoolboy age, his sketchbook drawings of places and artefacts that later crop up in the *Rynosseros* series—is, like the Tom stories themselves, truly marvelous.

The PS *Complete Rynosseros* is a concinnity indeed—a skillful and harmonious fitting together of the different parts of something, for which diehard *Rynosseros* fans have waited, lo! these three-and-a-half decades, and for which all lovers of the surrealistic, the imaginative, and the fantastic should be eternally grateful. The glorious jacket artwork by Nick Stathopoulos that graces these editions is the crowning touch to these immaculately presented editions of Dowling's magnum opus.

About the Contributors

Michael Abolafia is a co-editor of *Dead Reckonings*.

Jonathan Berman is a filmmaker and professor (Cal State San Marcos) whose work explores subculture and identity, redefining how alternative people, groups, and ideas are represented. Films include *My Friend Paul* (1999), about mental illness, friendship, and crime; *Commune* (2006), about a seminal experiment in group living; and *Calling All Earthlings* (2018), about George Van Tassel and his desert wonder dome, the Integratron.

Leigh Blackmore is the official editor of the international Sword and Sorcery and Weird Fiction Terminus amateur press association. His recent weird verse has appeared in issues of *Penumbra* and in the *Speculations III* anthology from Mind's Eye Publications. Forthcoming work includes the liner notes for a vinyl record album from Cadabra Records, and his occult thriller novel *The Eighth Trigram*. Leigh runs his own copyediting and manuscript assessment company, Proof Perfect Editorial Services, based in the Illawarra region, NSW.

Ramsey Campbell is an English horror fiction writer, editor, and critic who has been writing for well over fifty years. He is frequently cited as one of the leading writers in the field. His website is www.ramseycampbell.com.

Philip Challinor has published several articles on the work of Robert Aickman, some of which were collected in the chapbook *Akin to Poetry* (2010). He posts satire, fiction, and assorted grumbles on a blog, *The Curmudgeon,* and his longer fiction is available at Lulu.com.

Greg Gbur is a professor of physics and optical science at UNCC Charlotte. For more than a decade he has written a blog called Skulls in the Stars (skullsinthestars.com) about physics, horror fiction, and curious intersections between them. He has written a number of introductions to classic re-printed horror novels for Valancourt Books.

Edward Guimont is assistant professor of world history at Bristol Community College in Fall River, Massachusetts. He has published several articles on Lovecraft's connections to Connecticut, the Arctic, and Mars, and is co-writing a book with Horace A. Smith on Lovecraft, astronomy, and space opera.

Alex Houstoun is a co-editor of *Dead Reckonings*. He has published *Copyright Questions and the Stories of H. P. Lovecraft,* available by contacting him at deadreckoningsjournal@gmail.com.

Javier A. Martinez was managing editor of *Extrapolation* for fifteen years. A former department chair, college dean, and university provost, he is currently professor of English in the Department of Literatures and Cultural Studies at the University of Texas Rio Grande Valley.

Michael D. Miller is a former professor of genre studies, currently active writing reviews, articles, and poetry for the weird fiction genre with work appearing in *Dead Reckonings, Lovecraft Annual, Spectral Realms, Penumbra, Alien Buddha Press, Dumpster Fire Press,* and *Marchxness*. He is the author of the *Realms of Fantasy PRG* for Mythopoeia Games Publications.

David Peak's cosmic horror novel *The World Below* was published by Apocalypse Party in March 2022. More information can be found at david-peak.com. He lives in Chicago.

Daniel Pietersen is the editor of *I Am Stone: The Gothic Weird Tales of R. Murray Gilchrist,* part of the British Library's Tales of the Weird series. He is also a regular guest lecturer for the Romancing the Gothic project.

June Pulliam teaches courses about slasher films and zombies at Louisiana State University in Baton Rouge, where she lives in an old house with multiple cats and dogs. She is the author of several books on subjects ranging from zombies to punk rock. When she is not dodging hurricanes, she paints.

Dr. Géza A. G. Reilly is a writer and critic with an interest in twentieth-century American genre literature. A Canadian expatriate, he now lives in the wilds of Florida with his wife, Andrea, and their cat, Mim.

A career-retrospective of **Darrell Schweitzer**'s short fiction was published by PS Publishing in two volumes in 2020. A veritable flood of Schweitzeriana is soon to follow from various publishers in the next year or so, including a new Lovecraftian anthology, *Shadows out of Time* (PS), *The Best of* Weird Tales: *The 1920s* (Centipede Press), *The Best of* Weird Tales *1924* (with John Betancourt, Wildside Press), a weird poetry collection, *Dancing Before Azathoth* (P'rea Press), a new story collection, *The Children of Chorazin* (Hippocampus Press), and two further volumes of author interviews (Wildside Press). He was co-editor of *Weird Tales* between 1988 and 2007.

Donald Sidney-Fryer is a poet, historian, entertainer, and one of the foremost experts on the work of Clark Ashton Smith. His latest book, *Astral Debris,* is forthcoming from Hippocampus Press.

www.ingramcontent.com/pod-product-compliance
Lightning Source LLC
Chambersburg PA
CBHW071822020426
42331CB00007B/1583